PLAYBOOK
on *OUR FATHER*

PLAYBOOK
on *OUR FATHER*

EMMAUS
ROAD
PUBLISHING

Steubenville, Ohio
A Division of Catholics United for the Faith
www.emmausroad.org

**Danny Abramowicz • Peter Herbeck
Brian Patrick • Curtis Martin**

Emmaus Road Publishing
827 North Fourth Street
Steubenville, Ohio 43952

Library of Congress Control Number: 2010931757
ISBN: 978-1-931018-66-1

Cover design and layout by
Theresa Westling

CONTENTS

Message from
COACH DANNY

The Crossing the Goal Ministries (CTG) was created as an outreach ministry to men out of concern for their spiritual wellbeing. I had personally been involved in Catholic Men's ministry for 25 years and I saw a growing need for resources adapted solely for men to challenge them to become spiritually fit.

For this reason, the CTG team began developing resources, first with a TV show, *Crossing the Goal*, which airs on EWTN television and radio and can be viewed online at www.crossingthegoal.com. Springing forth from the shows came DVDs based on the various episodes. We then designed a *Playbook* from the content of the shows to work in conjunction with the DVDs. These can be used either personally or in a group setting, which we call Spiritual Fitness Workouts.

Now, let me give you a breakdown of each of these various CTG resources so that you can get a better understanding of what they are and how they work as a unit.

CTG—SHOW

❑   The weekly program for men airs on EWTN and radio.

❑   The show's set and format has a sports theme comparable to ESPN Sportscenter and NFL Today.

❑   The show has four segments:
    ❑ **"Kickoff"**—the team introduces the topic.

    ❑ **"Game Plan"**—we go more in depth about the subject matter.

- ❏ **"Red Zone"**—we personalize the topic.
- ❏ **"End Zone"**—each team member gives the viewers an action item to work on for the next week.

❏ The shows are based on (and faithful to) the teachings of the Catholic Church, and use Scripture and the Catechism as sources.

❏ Some of the basic topics covered on these shows: the virtues, the parts of the Our Father, the roles of a man (father, son, warrior, etc.), the seven deadly sins, characteristics of a godly man.

❏ Each topic is broken down into 8 to 10 episodes that make up a series.

CTG—DVD

❏ Each series of the show—such as "The Virtues" and "The Our Father"—is edited and placed on DVDs.

❏ Each episode of the series has approximately 25 minutes of content.

CTG—*PLAYBOOK*

❏ The *Playbook* was designed by the CTG team to work in conjunction with the DVDs.

❏ The *Playbook* has sections similar to the TV show's various segments:
  - ❏ **"Kickoff"**—introduction of the topic
  - ❏ **"Game Plan"**—better understanding of the topic
  - ❏ **"Red Zone"**—personalizes the topic
  - ❏ **"End Zone"**—personal action plan

❏ There are three additional features:
  - ❏ **"Pregame"**—brief reading prepares the mind and heart
  - ❏ **"Time Out"**—questions for the men to reflect on and hopefully share their answers with one another in a group setting
  - ❏ **"Halftime"**—this section is for personal reflection, either at the meeting or at home.

❏ Additional *Playbooks* and DVDs can be ordered through the CTG website, www.crossingthegoal.com

CTG—SPIRITUAL FITNESS WORKOUT GROUPS

What are Spiritual Fitness Workouts?

Spiritual Fitness Workout Groups are 15 to 50 men who meet once a week for 90 minutes, using the CTG DVDs and Playbooks as discussion guides to aid them in their spiritual growth.

Mission

To train and strengthen ourselves inwardly through these workouts so that we become Godly men, who will make a positive difference in our homes, parishes, workplaces, and communities.

Purpose

1. To gather men together to honor God in prayer and worship.

2. To invite the Holy Spirit to penetrate our hearts to change us interiorly.

3. To educate ourselves through the teachings of the Catholic Church utilizing the Scriptures and the Catechism.

4. To share with one another how God is working in each of our lives on a daily basis.

5. To recruit and encourage other men to join us in spiritual training and workouts.

Goal

To mobilize men to actively engage the mission of the church.

How to set up
Spiritual Fitness Workout Groups

Follow these steps to set up Workout Groups in your parish:

Step 1: LEADERSHIP

❑ Two or three key men in the parish will make up the core leadership team.

❑ Choose two men to be the initial workout leaders.

❑ As you grow, encourage others to become more involved in leadership roles.

Step 2: APPROVAL

❑ Set an appointment with the pastor to get his approval and to ask him to join you in the workouts as a participant. Make sure the deacons are included.

❑ Make sure you understand the mission, purpose, and goal for the Spiritual Fitness Workout before meeting with the pastor.

❑ Be prepared to explain to the pastor the format of the workouts and the benefits to the parish.

Step 3: LOCATION

❑ Parish: choose a meeting room in the parish center that gives you some privacy and the ability to expand.

❑ Make sure the area you choose can accommodate a TV monitor.

❑ Homes are very nice but they limit the size of the group and are a huge commitment.

Step 4: SCHEDULE AND FORMAT

❏   Schedule: Workouts are held weekly (90 minutes).

Examples: Thursdays, 7:30–9:00 p.m. or
           Saturdays, 7:00–8:30 a.m. or
           Tuesdays after 6:30 a.m. Mass

Topic	Time
Prayer and Accountability	
Welcome and prayer	5 minutes
Praise and Worship (2 to 3 songs)	10 minutes
General Sharing (Accountability): Small groups of 5 to 7 men review previous week's personal action plans.	10 minutes
	Subtotal: 25 minutes
Video and Discussion *Watch CTG show by segment, with small group discussions of 5 to 7 men following each segment.*	
Segment 1: "Kickoff" and "Game Plan." DVD 10 min. followed by 15 min. sharing.	25 minutes
Segment 2: "Red Zone." DVD 10 min. followed by 25 min sharing.	35 minutes
Segment 3: "End Zone." DVD 3 min. followed by personal action plan 2 min.	5 minutes
	Subtotal: 65 minutes
Closing prayer (brief)	

Step 5: EQUIPMENT AND MATERIALS

❏ Each person should bring *CTG Playbook* and Bible—have one copy of the Catechism on hand.

❏ Leader is responsible for providing:
   o CTG DVD
   o music sheets and CD player for worship and praise songs
   o TV monitor and DVD player for teaching

Step 6: PROMOTION

❏ All men are welcome.

❏ Take advantage of regional CTG conferences: approach organizers to have your group and membership sign-ups announced.

❏ Make an announcement from the pulpit at Mass; use the parish bulletin.

❏ Word of mouth seems to work the best and it is the most personal and effective.

❏ Place CTG posters in high-traffic areas.

❏ Use business-like calling cards.

Step 7: WORKOUT GROUP LEADER RESPONSIBILITIES

❏ Prepare for each meeting (for example, preview the CTG episode).

- ❏ Make sure the room is properly set up.

- ❏ Double-check all of the equipment. Make sure the TV and DVD are properly connected. Have a CD player on hand for the music.

- ❏ Have designated facilitators (see Step 9 for Facilitators duties) who can lead the small group discussions planned for each meeting.

- ❏ Find several guys who can take turns opening and closing the meeting rooms.

- ❏ Refreshments are sometimes supplied by the parish, but more than likely an offering should be taken to purchase soft drinks, coffee, cookies, etc.

- ❏ *Everyone* makes sure the room is placed back in order.

Step 8: GROWTH

- ❏ Try to follow up with a phone call to each new member you bring to the meeting. Make sure everything is O.K. and remind him of the next meeting.

- ❏ Be aware of men that are "no-shows" and let them know they are missed.

- ❏ Each man should invite and bring one new man per month, and then follow through by encouraging him to keep coming back with a personal invite by you.

Step 9: TIPS FOR FACILITATORS

- ❏ Create a "safe place." Everything said in the group stays in the group and is held in *strict confidence.*

- ❏ Keep everything moving. If the discussion lags, move on to the next question. Keep an eye on the clock.

- ❏ Stay on the subject at hand. Don't get off base.

- ❑ Don't allow one person to dominate the sharing. You must kindly interrupt so the group can move on.

- ❑ You don't need to comment on the men's answers to the discussion questions.

- ❑ All members, and their sharing, are of equal value. No gurus.

- ❑ Discussion of public figures and issues should be discouraged. It is not a debating session.

- ❑ Discussion of Church figures and issues should be discouraged.

- ❑ Personal counseling during the meetings should be avoided.

- ❑ Personal experiences can be shared, but any major issues should be handled outside of the meeting.

- ❑ Sensitive and difficult disclosures and sharing can be followed by taking time out to pray.

- ❑ Be sensitive to the movement of the Holy Spirit and flexible to follow that movement.

- ❑ Start and stop *on time*.

COACHING POINTS FOR A GREAT WORKOUT

- ❑ Come properly prepared for each workout.
- ❑ Bring your *Playbook* and Bible to each workout.
- ❑ Make a committed effort to accomplish your action item for the week.
- ❑ Ask the Holy Spirit to make you more open to sharing.
- ❑ Honor your commitment to the Lord by attending each weekly workout.

HOW TO USE THIS PLAYBOOK

- Bring the *Playbook* and Bible to each and every workout.

- The *Playbook* includes whitespace for taking notes. The men should take notes as they watch each segment.

- The Workout Leader starts the workout by showing the group the first two segments of the DVD: "Kickoff" and "Game Plan."

- The large group then breaks into smaller groups of five to seven men each and appoints one facilitator for each group.

- Open the *Playbook* to "Time Out" (after "Game Plan") which has questions that can help and encourage each man to share his answers with his group. This portion of sharing lasts *15 minutes.*

- The "Halftime" section is for personal reflection, either at the meeting or at home.

- The Workout Leader then shows the next segment of the DVD, "Red Zone," to all the men.

- The men break into small groups and again answer and discuss questions in "Time Out" (after "Red Zone"). This portion of sharing lasts *25 minutes.*

- The Workout Leader shows the last segment of the DVD, "End Zone," and then gives the men two minutes to write down an "action plan" for the next week.

- The action plan will be discussed at the beginning of the following week's workout. The reason for this sharing is accountability. This portion of sharing lasts *10 minutes.*

- Homework—The *Playbook* should be taken home to review and reflect on the things that were covered during the prior workout.

Glossary of Football Terms

- ## Kickoff
  A kick that begins play at the start of a football game.

- ## Game Plan
  Preparation and strategy for a team to defeat an opponent.

- ## Halftime
  Period between halves for reinforcing and adjusting the game plan.

- ## Red Zone
  A critical area from the opponent's 20-yard line to their goal line.

- ## End Zone
  The area you must enter to score a touchdown.

Coaching objectives for each segment

- ## Kickoff
  Let's get off to a great start with good field position concerning our spiritual goals.

- ## Game Plan
  We must prepare ourselves properly for the struggles that we will face in our everyday life.

- ## Halftime
  Review and adjust our plan and get ready for our march to the goal line.

- ## Red Zone
  Each one of us must be totally focused and alert for the tactics of our opponent (the devil).

- ## End Zone
  Don't be satisfied with just a field goal—we want to score a touchdown.

THE OUR FATHER

The version of the Our Father we usually pray is in Matthew. Jesus gave it to us in the Sermon on the Mount, and if we look at it in context we can learn a lot about how He wants us to pray:

And in praying do not heap up empty phrases as the Gentiles do; for they think that they will be heard for their many words. Do not be like them, for your Father knows what you need before you ask him.
Pray then like this:

Our Father who art in heaven,
Hallowed be thy name.
Thy kingdom come,
Thy will be done,
On earth as it is in heaven.
Give us this day our daily bread;
And forgive us our trespasses,
As we forgive those who trespass against us;
And lead us not into temptation,
But deliver us from evil.

For if you forgive men their trespasses, your heavenly Father also will forgive you; but if you do not forgive men their trespasses, neither will your Father forgive your trespasses.

(Matthew 6:7–15)

Our Father Who Art in Heaven

Brian Patrick

PRE-GAME

We call this prayer the "Our Father" because those are the first two words in it. We're praying to our Father. But what kind of Father do we have in heaven?

When Jesus explained what the Father was like to His followers, He used stories and pictures to help them understand, even if only a little. The reality is far beyond anything we can imagine. But He told this story to help us get some idea of how the Father feels about us:

> There was a man who had two sons; and the younger of them said to his father, "Father, give me the share of property that falls to me." And he divided his living between them.
>
> Not many days later, the younger son gathered all he had and took his journey into a far country, and there he squandered his property in loose living. And when he had spent everything, a great famine arose in that country, and he began to be in want. So he went and joined himself to one of the citizens of that country, who sent him into his fields to feed swine. And he would gladly have fed on the pods that the swine ate; and no one gave him anything.
>
> But when he came to himself he said, "How many of my father's hired servants have bread enough and to spare, but I perish here with hunger! I will arise and go to my father, and I will say to him, 'Father, I have sinned against heaven and before you; I am no longer worthy to be called your son; treat me as one of your hired servants.'"

And he arose and came to his father.

But while he was yet at a distance, his father saw him and had compassion, and ran and embraced him and kissed him.

And the son said to him, "Father, I have sinned against heaven and before you; I am no longer worthy to be called your son."

But the father said to his servants, "Bring quickly the best robe, and put it on him; and put a ring on his hand, and shoes on his feet; and bring the fatted calf and kill it, and let us eat and make merry; for this my son was dead, and is alive again; he was lost, and is found." And they began to make merry.

Now his elder son was in the field; and as he came and drew near to the house, he heard music and dancing. And he called one of the servants and asked what this meant.

And he said to him, "Your brother has come, and your father has killed the fatted calf, because he has received him safe and sound."

But he was angry and refused to go in.

His father came out and entreated him, but he answered his father, "Behold, these many years I have served you, and I never disobeyed your command; yet you never gave me a kid, that I might make merry with my friends. But when this son of yours came, who has devoured your living with harlots, you killed for him the fatted calf!"

And he said to him, "Son, you are always with me, and all that is mine is yours. It was fitting to make merry and be glad, for this your brother was dead, and is alive; he was lost, and is found."

(Luke 15:11–32)

KICKOFF

1. We need to reflect on every word of the Our Father.

2. It's an intimate look into the heart of Jesus.

3. The Apostles saw in Jesus' life the difference that prayer made.

4. The Our Father teaches us not only what to pray but how to pray.

5. Seven petitions: seven habits of the heart that Jesus wants us to develop, which will lead to success not only in this life but also in eternal life.

6. Slow down and think about the words.

7. Catholics sometimes have a hard time praying to the Father; we're more comfortable with Jesus.

8. The first word, "Our," stresses the communal nature of the prayer.

GAME PLAN

1. The Our Father comes in the middle of the Sermon on the Mount. The theme of the Sermon on the Mount is fatherhood.

2. The Father is what it's all about. Jesus came to reveal the Father.

3. When Adam fell, something died in the human heart: trust in the Father.

4. Jesus' mission is to reveal the Father to a race that has lost sight of Him.

5. The parable of the Prodigal Son shows two brothers who misunderstand the Father. One rebels; one acts as a slave. The Father wants neither rebellion nor slavery: He wants our hearts.

6. To see Jesus is to see the Father—love, healing, and deliverance.

7. Jesus on the Cross expresses to the world the nature of the Father, which is love.

8. The idea of God as a Father is radical: God rules the universe with the heart of a Father.

9. Jesus also communicates with the Father with the heart of a loyal Son: "Father, I want to give you what my brothers and sisters have failed to give you forever. I want to return the love to you that you deserve   to give to God what belongs to God."

10. The Cross is brutal. Jesus knows it will be tough, but He's willing to endure it to show us how far we can go in trusting the Father.

11. The message of the Cross is Jesus living what He taught about the Father.

12. Man does not live by bread alone, but by the words of the Father. The Father's words are life to us.

13. As adults, we need to recognize the depth of the prayer we learned as children.

GAME PLAN SUMMARY

- The Father wants neither rebellion nor slavery: He wants our hearts.
- Jesus shows us how to give to God what belongs to God.
- Be ready to recognize the depth of the Our Father.

TIME OUT

Warm-up questions

1. What particular point(s) caught your attention the most in this segment?

_____

_____

_____

_____

_____

_____

_____

2. What is something useful that you learned from viewing this segment that you can apply in your own life?

_____

_____

_____

_____

_____

_____

_____

Workout questions

1. How does the image of Jesus on the Cross reveal the Father's love?

_____

_____

_____

_____

_____

_____

2. What can we learn from Jesus' relationship with His Father?

_____

_____

_____

_____

_____

_____

_____

HALFTIME

The Our Father appears twice in the Gospels—once in Matthew and once in Luke. The version in Matthew is what we commonly memorize. The version in Luke is slightly different; and it was given to the disciples at a different time, when one of the disciples asked Jesus to show them how to pray. In response, the Lord gave them this version of the Our Father. He also taught them a little about praying, giving them examples of how asking for things works even in the human world.

He was praying in a certain place, and when he ceased, one of his disciples said to him, "Lord, teach us to pray, as John taught his disciples."

And he said to them, "When you pray, say:

'Father, hallowed be your name.

Your kingdom come.

Give us each day our daily bread;

and forgive us our sins, for we ourselves forgive every one who is indebted to us;

and lead us not into temptation.'"

And he said to them, "Which of you who has a friend will go to him at midnight and say to him, 'Friend, lend me three loaves; for a friend of mine has arrived on a journey, and I have nothing to set before him'; and he will answer from within, 'Do not bother me; the door is now shut, and my children are with me in bed; I cannot get up and give you anything'? I tell you, though he will not get up and give him anything because he is his friend, yet because of his importunity he will rise and give him whatever he needs.

And I tell you, Ask, and it will be given you; seek, and you will find; knock, and it will be opened to you. For every one who asks receives, and he who seeks finds, and to him who knocks it will be opened.

What father among you, if his son asks for a fish, will instead of a fish give him a serpent; or if he asks for an egg, will give him a scorpion? If you then, who are evil, know how to give good gifts to your children, how much more will the heavenly Father give the Holy Spirit to those who ask him!" (Luke 11:1–13)

RED ZONE // RED ZONE

1. Many people don't know how to relate to the Father. Is he a capricious judge, remote, impossible to please?

2. The human heart has been wounded: we don't trust the Father. We even blame Him for things.

3. We have free will. We have no one but ourselves to blame for our bad choices.

4. God brings us back with love and care.

5. He works through other people to bring us back.

6. We're hardwired with the desire to receive from our fathers.

7. God is the perfect Father.

8. Why do bad things happen to good people? Is God really a loving Father?

9. We messed up the world. We can't get along with one another; we're greedy.

10. God is all-powerful and all good.

11. We love and serve a God so powerful that He can draw good out of evil.

12. The greatest evil in history was the murder of Jesus Christ. From that God draws the salvation of the world.

13. We need our Father's approval.

14. How do you get a real relationship with the Father?

15. Sometimes having our own children can give us a sense of what God is like. We love them no matter what, as God loves us.

16. Nobody's perfect, but God still loves us.

17. God reveals Himself through Scripture. The Scriptures reveal the perfect Father-Son relationship.

RED ZONE // RED ZONE

TIME OUT

Warm-up questions

1. What particular point(s) caught your attention the most in this segment?

_____

_____

_____

_____

_____

_____

2. What is something useful that you learned from viewing this segment that you can apply in your own life?

_____

_____

_____

_____

_____

_____

_____

Workout questions

1. Name some of the times in your life that God the Father has blessed you.

_____

_____

_____

_____

_____

_____

_____

2. How do you show God the Father your appreciation?

_____

_____

_____

_____

_____

_____

3. Danny mentioned that he chose the wrong road on many occasions that offended the Father. Share a particular occasion when you offended the Father through a poor decision.

_____

_____

_____

_____

_____

_____

_____

4. Name at least one time where your earthly father has been a blessing to you. When has he been a disappointment to you?

_____

_____

_____

_____

_____

_____

_____

5. Name at least one time when being a father has blessed you.

_____

_____

_____

_____

_____

_____

"Show me the Father."

➤ The only way to see who the Father is is to see Jesus.

➤ Read the passion narratives in Scripture (Mt. 26–27; Mk. 14–15; Lk. 22–23; Jn. 18–19).

➤ As you read, say, "Jesus, show me the Father."

➤ What the Father said about Jesus is what He wants to say about us.

Our relationship with God is most important.

➤ We spend a lot of time trying to get wealth and climb the ladder.

➤ We could miss on all those other things and end up in a good relationship with the Father, and our life will be a complete success.

➤ Get everything you want, but without a relationship with the Father you're a complete failure.

➤ Our Father is a King, and you are His son.

COACHING POINT

Study Psalm 139

➤ Think about it, talk about it, turn it over in your heart.

➤ The Father will reveal Himself to you.

Psalm 139

To the choirmaster. A Psalm of David.
O Lᴏʀᴅ, you have searched me and known me!
You know when I sit down and when I rise up;
 you discern my thoughts from afar.
You search out my path and my lying down,
 and are acquainted with all my ways.
Even before a word is on my tongue,
 behold, O Lᴏʀᴅ, you know it altogether.
You beset me behind and before,
 and lay your hand upon me.
Such knowledge is too wonderful for me;
 it is high, I cannot attain it.
Where shall I go from your Spirit?
 Or where shall I flee from your presence?
If I ascend to heaven, your are there!
 If I make my bed in Sheol, you are there!
If I take the wings of the morning
 and dwell in the uttermost parts of the sea,

even there your hand shall lead me,
and your right hand shall hold me.
If I say, "Let only darkness cover me,
and the light about me be night,"
even the darkness is not dark to you,
the night is bright as the day;
for darkness is as light with you.
For you formed my inward parts,
you knit me together in my mother's womb.
I praise you, for I am wondrously made.
Wonderful are your works!
You know me right well;
my frame was not hidden from you,
when I was being made in secret,
intricately wrought in the depths of the earth.
Your eyes beheld my unformed substance;
in your book were written, every one of them,
the days that were formed for me,
when as yet there was none of them.
How precious to me are your thoughts, O God!
How vast is the sum of them!
If I would count them, they are more than the sand.
When I awake, I am still with you.
O that you would slay the wicked, O God,
and that men of blood would depart from me,
men who maliciously defy you,
who lift themselves up against you for evil!
Do I not hate them that hate you, O LORD?
And do I not loathe them that rise up against you?
I hate them with perfect hatred;
I count them my enemies.
Search me, O God, and know my heart!
Try me and know my thoughts!
And see if there be any wicked way in me,
and lead me in the way everlasting!

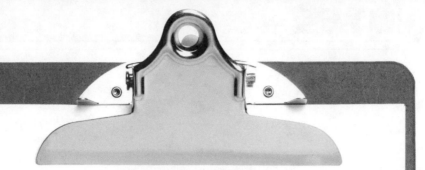

2 Minute Drill:
Personal Fitness Action Plan

Write out an action plan—I commit to becoming spiritually fit by...

NOTES

Hallowed Be
Thy Name

Brian Patrick

PRE-GAME

If you read the Bible in English, you may have noticed how the word "Lord" sometimes appears in small capitals—LORD—in the Old Testament.

That's not just some sort of fancy printer's trick. You see the word "Lord" in small capitals where the Hebrew text uses the name of God.

In Hebrew, God's name is "Yahweh," which means "I am." (Hebrew is written without .vowels, so we sometimes see the Name of God transliterated as "YHWH.")

You remember the story of the burning bush: God appeared to Moses in the desert and told him to go lead Israel out of Egypt. But Moses wasn't sure anyone would believe him.

> Then Moses said to God, "If I come to the sons of Israel and say to them, 'The God of your fathers has sent me to you,' and they ask me, 'What is his name?' what shall I say to them?"
> God said to Moses, "I AM WHO I AM." And he said, "Say this to the sons of Israel, 'I AM has sent me to you.'"
>
> (Exodus 3:13–14)

"Yahweh" was a name so holy that the Israelites wouldn't even speak it—not even when they were reading Scripture.

Whenever a Scripture reader would come across the name "Yahweh," he would say the Hebrew word for "the Lord" instead.

Now, speaking the Lord's name in the context of reading Scripture hardly seems to us like "taking the name of the Lord your God in vain." But the Israelites weren't taking any chances. If taking God's name in vain is breaking one of the Ten Commandments, then it was better not to speak the name at all than to break that commandment, even accidentally.

Most Christians don't go to such extremes to keep the Second Commandment. But we should remember the commandment every time we pray, "hallowed be thy name." It really is *that* important.

KICKOFF

1. In our society, the name of the Lord is thrown around like garbage.

2. Taking the name of the Lord in vain is a violation of one of the Ten Commandments.

3. We have to recognize that we're not only to *avoid breaking* the commandment, but we're also to *do something*.

4. Jesus Himself was zealous for the honor of His Father's name.

5. He's bringing us into His own disposition, to turn our hearts to the Father.

6. That begins with honoring God as holy.

7. We're not in awe of God anymore. When societies take God out of the equation, it doesn't work.

8. We may be embarrassed to be Catholic, to be Christian.

9. Jesus wants to share the awe of the Father with us.

10. Jesus died for the honor of the Father. He gave to the Father what belongs to the Father: obedience, trust, and surrender.

11. "If you deny me," Jesus said, "I'll deny you" That's scary.

12. It's significant that Jesus put this petition at the top of the Lord's Prayer.

The Second Commandment

You shall not take the name of the LORD your God in vain; for the LORD will not hold him guiltless who takes his name in vain.

(Exodus 20:7)

GAME PLAN

1. In the Second Commandment, we often overlook "for the Lord will not leave him unpunished" (or "hold him guiltless").

2. We go through periods in history when we believe taking the Lord's name in vain is no big deal.

3. But we *won't go unpunished.* The warning is supposed to get our attention.

4. God's name is holy because God is holy, great, awesome, and different from us—we are creatures, and He's the Creator.

5. It's healthy for us—we can live well—if we understand the difference between God and us.

6. Our ultimate problem is shrinking God and making God in *our* image.

7. Remember Jesus cleansing the temple—His blood started to boil. "You're not going to dishonor my Father."

8. We need to see that we bear the name of Christ and we radiate the love of God out to the rest of the world.

9. We hallow His name in our actions and words. We have to live transformed lives.

10. We're struggling for wisdom. "Fear of the Lord is the beginning of wisdom." Not slavish fear, but appropriate respect, awe, and overwhelming recognition.

11. Our souls are like gardens out of control. We have to pull out the weeds of bad habits—taking God's name in vain.

12. Then we have to plant what we want to grow: using God's name in a sacred manner.

13. We need to tell our kids, "You're welcome to use God's name when you're talking to Him, or when you're talking about Him."

14. Jesus died to give us the *Holy* Spirit—to give us new hearts.

15. Our hearts aren't ordered to the Father the way they should be, but the Holy Spirit changes that.

16. We have to have a certain zeal as men. People aren't conscious of attacking God because they've fallen into bad habits.

17. If you dishonor God, you'll dishonor the things of God. Look at how marriage is dishonored.

18. It starts with dishonoring the Creator.

19. Romans 1—suppressing the reality of God. (We'll look at Romans 1 during halftime.)

20. If we suppress the knowledge of God, our lives unravel.

21. The way out of our problems is to hallow His name.

GAME PLAN SUMMARY

- Understand the difference between God and us.
- Weed out the bad habit of taking God's name in vain.
- Get into the habit of using God's name in a sacred manner.

TIME OUT

Warm-up questions

1. What particular point(s) caught your attention the most in this segment?

_____

_____

HALLOWED BE THY NAME

_____

_____

_____

_____

_____

_____

2. What is something useful that you learned from viewing this segment that you can apply in your own life?

_____

_____

_____

_____

_____

_____

_____

Workout questions

1. Why do you think so many people in our society today reject the name of the Lord?

_____

_____

_____

_____

_____

_____

2. How much honor do we give to athletes, movie and rock stars, politicians, etc; and, on the other hand, how much honor and respect do we give to God?

_____

_____

_____

_____

_____

_____

_____

> The Passover of the Jews was at hand, and Jesus went up to Jerusalem. In the temple he found those who were selling oxen and sheep and pigeons, and the money-changers at their business.
>
> And making a whip of cords, he drove them all, with the sheep and oxen, out of the temple; and he poured out the coins of the money-changers and overturned their tables. And he told those who sold the pigeons, "Take these things away; you shall not make my Father's house a house of trade."
>
> His disciples remembered that it was written, "Zeal for your house will consume me."
>
> The Jews then said to him, "What sign have you to show us for doing this?"
>
> Jesus answered them, "Destroy this temple, and in three days I will raise it up.
>
> The Jews then said, "It has taken forty-six years to build this temple, and will you raise it up in three days?"
>
> But he spoke of the temple of his body. When therefore he was raised from the dead, his disciples remembered that he had said this; and they believed the scripture and the word which Jesus had spoken.
>
> (John 2:13–22)

HALFTIME

For the wrath of God is revealed from heaven against all ungodliness and wickedness of men who by their wickedness suppress the truth. For what can be known about God is plain to them, because God has shown it to them. Ever since the creation of the world his invisible nature, namely, his eternal power and deity, has been clearly perceived in the things that have been made. So they are without excuse; for although they knew God they did not honor him as God or give thanks to him, but they became futile in their thinking and their senseless minds were darkened. Claiming to be wise, they became fools, and exchanged the glory of the immortal God for images resembling mortal man or birds or animals or reptiles.

Therefore God gave them up in the lusts of their hearts to impurity, to the dishonoring of their bodies among themselves, because they exchanged the truth about God for a lie and worshiped and served the creature rather than the Creator, who is blessed for ever! Amen.

For this reason God gave them up to dishonorable passions. Their women exchanged natural relations for unnatural, and the men likewise gave up natural relations with women and were consumed with passion for one another, men committing shameless acts with men and receiving in their own persons the due penalty for their error.

And since they did not see fit to acknowledge God, God gave them up to a base mind and to improper conduct. They were filled with all manner of wickedness, evil, covetousness, malice. Full of envy, murder, strife, deceit, malignity, they are gossips, slanderers, haters of God, insolent, haughty, boastful, inventors of evil, disobedient to parents, foolish, faithless, heartless, ruthless. Though they know God's decree that those who do such things deserve to die, they not only do them but approve those who practice them.

(Romans 1:18–32

1. "Oh my God" is thrown around like it's nothing. What's the big deal? We may not see that it's a big deal, but using God's name like that violates the Second Commandment. If God said this was important, we need to take it seriously.

2. How often do we use God's name the *proper* way? "God bless you." That shocks people.

3. In the prayer, Jesus helps us develop the habit of placing ourselves under His purpose for us. This is going to need to be a priority for you because it's really big.

4. If you pray it every day, eventually you'll get a heart that wants and desires what's in the prayer. You'll start seeing why it's important. Before you know it, you'll start blessing people.

5. Think of how we hallow athletes, movies stars, and politicians, but we can't give God the time of day. We're like ants overwhelmed by another ant that we see, but we don't notice God.

6. Jesus says you need to hallow the Father's name on the inside.

7. Then we, as men, need to hallow His name in the culture.

8. If we hear someone taking the Lord's name in vain, it's appropriate to say "Excuse me, I'd appreciate it if you wouldn't use that language." Wake people up. We're living in a culture that's becoming more and more hostile to Jesus.

9. We're sensitive toward respecting other people, but not toward respecting the Lord. If you have respect for the Lord, you're going to have respect for other people.

10. We shouldn't have unenlightened, inappropriate zeal, like the assassin who murdered Van Gogh's nephew for misusing the name of Allah. But there is an *appropriate,* enlightened zeal that Jesus had.

11. We men in the Church today are very wimpy. The Lord's name and the things of God are dishonored and thrown in the dirt, but very few men stand up to defend them. We'll continue to get stepped on until we stand up.

12. We're not to kill for Christ, but to live for Him. Jesus didn't defend Himself when He went to the Cross, but His blood boiled when His Father's name was dishonored in the temple.

13. He took action because He wanted to teach His disciples, "You do not dishonor my Father or the things of the Father."

14. We believe in God, but when do we stand up? If not now, when? Our Church is under attack. Our God is under attack. If you believe in God, stand up. How much worse does it have to get?

15. WAKE UP or WIMP OUT.

16. We're not proud of the people who stood by and did nothing while Hitler came to power. We rightly praise folks like Martin Luther King who did the right thing when bad things were happening.

17. Well, don't just praise him. Go out and imitate him. Do the right thing when bad things are happening.

18. Use your gifts. If people are writing books dishonoring God, and you have that gift, write a book that answers them. If people dishonor God in office conversation, stand up and tell the truth.

19. Who's behind all this? The devil.

20. Two things you don't ever talk about: your faith and politics. You *should* talk about them.

21. When do we find time to talk about the Lord?

22. We hallow His name in our words and actions. When we speak, we honor the Father. When we act, we won't stand by idly when other people dishonor the Father.

23. Marriage is dishonored today. Why? Partly because we dishonor God. If you don't respect God, you don't respect the things of God.

24. God created us in His image. If we lose that, we get it back by *hallowing God's name.*

TIME OUT

Warm-up questions

1. What particular point(s) caught your attention the most in this segment?

_____

_____

_____

_____

_____

_____

2. What is something useful that you learned from viewing this segment that you can apply in your own life?

_____

_____

_____

_____

_____

_____

_____

Workout questions

1. Give some examples of how you hallow God's name not only by your words but also by your actions.

_____

_____

_____

_____

_____

_____

_____

2. Think of the most recent times that you took God's name in vain (e.g., g--d---). What caused you to do this? (e.g., anger, frustration)

_____

_____

_____

_____

_____

_____

_____

3. When you hear someone at work take the name of God in vain, what is your reaction?

_____

_____

_____

_____

_____

_____

_____

4. If our society is becoming more and more hostile to the name of the Lord and Christians in general, what should your response to this be as a man of God?

_____

_____

_____

_____

_____

_____

_____

Stand up for the Lord.

➤ The whole Church is waiting for men of God to stand up and honor the Father.

➤ Look for opportunities this week to stand up and honor the name of the Lord.

Catechism 2666

➤ Plant the flag right now: "Today and the rest of my life, I will not dishonor the name of the Lord."

➤ If you've developed the habit of misusing God's name, rip that habit out.

➤ The name of Jesus will lead you to the Father.

➤ If someone on TV uses the name of the Lord in vain, get up and turn it off. Or at least change the channel. Say "Not in my house."

The Name above all names (Catechism 2666)

But the one name that contains everything is the one that the Son of God received in his incarnation: JESUS. The divine name may not be spoken by human lips, but by assuming our humanity The Word of God hands it over to us and we can invoke it: "Jesus," "YHWH saves." (Cf. E.g., 3:14; 33:19–23; Mt. 1:21.) The name "Jesus" contains all: God and man and the whole economy of creation and salvation. To pray "Jesus" is to invoke him and to call him within us. His name is the only one that contains the presence it signifies. Jesus is the Risen One, and whoever invokes the name of Jesus is welcoming the Son of God who loved him and who gave himself up for him (Rom. 10:13; Acts 2:21; 3:15-16; Gal. 2:20).

Catechism, no. 2666

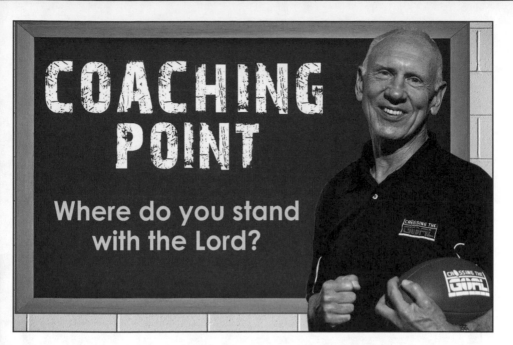

➤ Reflect on how many blessings God has given you.

➤ Then think how many times you've hurt God or not stood up for the Lord.

➤ You be the judge. You'll find out where you stand with the Lord.

2 Minute Drill:
Personal Fitness Action Plan

Write out an action plan—I commit to becoming spiritually fit by…

NOTES

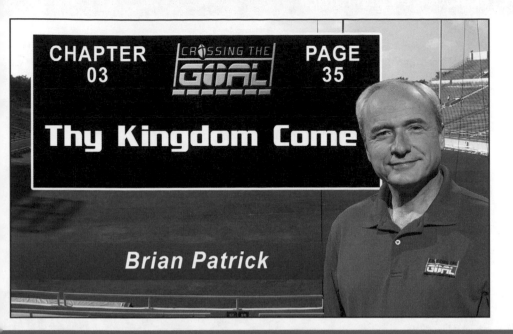

PRE-GAME

It wasn't easy being a Founding Father.

Back in 1775, only a few hotheads in the American colonies talked about permanently separating from Great Britain.

It just didn't seem reasonable. Why rock the boat that much? After all, most of the people in the colonies had been British all their lives. True, the British government wasn't treating them very well, but surely that could be fixed. A new government in England would see reason, and everything would be fine. Best just to stick it out.

But by the middle of 1776 there was strong support for an independent American nation. There were cheers everywhere as the Declaration of Independence was announced.

What happened?

Well, in many ways the British government made the argument for independence itself. By becoming more and more repressive—more obviously evil—the government made the Americans more and more conscious of what a good government *should* be like.

The people felt as though they were being treated like slaves. If they couldn't get good government from Britain, then they would have to design it on their own.

The Founding Fathers had a vision of a great nation where the government worked for the people. They clearly saw the problems with the kingdom they were living in, and they knew it was going to take a clean break to fix them.

Even when they couldn't see the details, they could see the big picture, and that was what they always worked for. They saw a country where every one of us could live in freedom, becoming the people we knew we could be.

It was a lot of work, with a lot of mistakes along the way. But they succeeded in breaking away from the kingdom of Great Britain and founding a great nation on the principles they believed in.

Well, you and I are locked in an even bigger battle between kingdoms.

The kingdom of the devil—"this world," as the Bible would call it—wants to keep us slaves forever.

The kingdom of God wants to set us free to become the people we know we can be.

Which one will you choose? Are you ready to send Satan your own declaration of independence?

KICKOFF

1. The New Testament is based on the Old Testament.

2. Matthew introduces Jesus as Son of David. That means He's king—heir to David.

3. David was promised that a king would come from his line who would rule all the nations for all time.

4. Jesus is the king of that universal, everlasting kingdom.

5. Colossians 1:13: We have been transferred from the kingdom of darkness to the kingdom of light.

6. There are two types of people: those who live in darkness and those who live in light.

7. People don't understand that. They live in this present time, and once this ends it's over. We don't have eternal perspective.

8. The kingdom is the king. Jesus Christ is the King; everything He is, said, and did communicates what the kingdom of God is like.

9. When the president comes on board his jet, that jet becomes Air Force One. In the same way, wherever Jesus is, there is the kingdom.

10. If we live the life of Christ, we extend that kingdom.

11. Then His kingdom comes as we take it into the world.

12. Ephesians 6:12 shows there's a battle between kingdoms. Whose side are we on?

13. There is nothing wrong with living in this world, but there is something wrong when we don't even think about God's kingdom.

14. The kingdom is here now, but it will be fulfilled and perfected in heaven.

15. Advance God's kingdom NOW—live that militant kingdom, the kingdom at war, and extend it in the hostile territory of the kingdom of darkness.

From darkness to light

May you be strengthened with all power, according to his glorious might, for all endurance and patience with joy, giving thanks to the Father, who has qualified us to share in the inheritance of the saints in light. He has delivered us from the dominion of darkness and transferred us to the kingdom of his beloved Son, in whom we have redemption, the forgiveness of sins.

(Colossians 1:11–14)

We're fighting the devil

Finally, be strong in the Lord and in the strength of his might. Put on the whole armor of God, that you may be able to stand against the wiles of the devil.

For we are not contending against flesh and blood, but against the principalities, against the powers, against the world rulers of this present darkness, against the spiritual hosts of wickedness in the heavenly places.

Therefore take the whole armor of God, that you may be able to withstand in the evil day, and having done all, to stand. Stand therefore, having fastened the belt of truth around your waist, and having put on the breastplate of righteousness, and having shod your feet with the equipment of the gospel of peace; besides all these, taking the shield of faith, with which you can quench all the flaming darts of the Evil One. And take the helmet of salvation, and the sword of the Spirit, which is the word of God.

(Ephesians 6:10–17)

GAME PLAN

1. Imagine two flags: the flag of the world and the flag of Christ. Whose flag will you pick?

2. We can have things of this world if we serve Christ, but we have to place the Lord at the center of our life—otherwise worldly things become an entanglement to us.

3. Jesus is a King and a Warrior. 1 John 3 says He came here to destroy the works of the devil.

4. Another rule was dominating us—we were under sin. Jesus came to break that hold on us so we could be free.

5. 1 Corinthians 15: God sent the Son to bring everything under right order under God.

6. The Church exists between the two comings of Jesus. He came first as a Lamb to call back the fallen world. He will come again in glory to judge the living and the dead, and *His kingdom will have no end.*

7. Jesus is at work right now subduing all the enemies of God—including my heart.

8. But we have freedom. If we refuse to come under His dominion, we end up in hell.

9. The Founding Fathers of the United States must have envisioned a new, great nation—it must have dominated their thoughts. If we think this battle between kingdoms is no big deal, we're really not patriots.

10. Christ calls for loyalty. There's a lot of work to be done.

11. Where is the kingdom of God? Wherever you can plant the flag of Jesus Christ and it's honored and respected.

12. Where it's dishonored, you find the "world"—the things that fight against the kingdom of God.

13. Fight to raise the flag of Christ in your heart and life.

14. We're not supposed to kill for Christ—we're supposed to live for Him, and if necessary die for Him.

15. The battle goes on in the liturgy, in the Mass.

16. When God's angels and saints gather in the Mass and pray to Christ, the kingdom comes.

17. When the saints and angels pray, the earth trembles. The principalities and powers are being shattered.

18. In the Eucharist, together in communion we acknowledge that Jesus Christ is Lord.

19. In our culture today, Christianity is dishonored. The world is turning hostile to Jesus Christ.

20. Get ready now for the spiritual battle ahead.

21. It's not going to get better unless men wake up spiritually and begin to live as kingdom builders.

22. The prayer "Thy kingdom come" says, "Lord, plant your flag in my heart. Transform me and bring my heart, mind, and will under your kingdom."

23. We'll meet people who disagree with us, but our battle isn't with them. It's with the spiritual powers of evil.

24. We're not fighting *against* people—we're fighting *for* people. People's souls are the prize at stake here.

25. We have to try to win every man, woman, and child for the kingdom.

26. The whole battle was won for us on the Cross.

27. We win the battle not by raising a sword against somebody, but by laying down our lives in love the way Jesus did.

The Son of God came to destroy the works of the devil

You know that he appeared to take away sins, and in him there is no sin. Any one who abides in him does not sin; any one who sins has not seen him, nor has he known him.

Little children, let no one deceive you. He who does right is righteous, as he is righteous. He who commits sin is of the devil; for the devil has sinned from the beginning. The reason the Son of God appeared was to destroy the works of the devil.

Any one born of God does not commit sin; for God's seed abides in him, and he cannot sin because he is born of God. By this it may be seen who are the children of God, and who are the children of the devil: whoever does not do right is not of God, nor he who does not love his brother.

(1 John 3:5–10)

He must reign

But in fact Christ has been raised from the dead, the first fruits of those who have fallen asleep. For as by a man came death, by a man has come also the resurrection of the dead. For as in Adam all die, so also in Christ shall all be made alive. But each in his own order: Christ the first fruits, then at his coming those who belong to Christ.

Then comes the end, when he delivers the kingdom to God the Father after destroying every rule and every authority and power. For he must reign until he has put all his enemies under his feet. The last enemy to be destroyed is death.

"For God has put all things in subjection under his feet." But when it says, "All things are put in subjection under him," it is plain that he is excepted who put all things under him. When all things are subjected to him, then the Son himself will also be subjected to him who put all things under him, that God may be everything to every one.

(1 Corinthians 15:20–28)

GAME PLAN SUMMARY

- Pick the flag of the kingdom you're going to serve.

- Raise the flag of Christ in your heart and in your life.

- We are not contending against flesh and blood but against principalities and powers.

TIME OUT

Warm-up questions

1. What particular point(s) caught your attention the most in this segment?

_____

_____

_____

_____

_____

_____

_____

2. What is something useful that you learned from viewing this segment that you can apply in your own life?

_____

_____

_____

_____

_____

_____

_____

Warm-up questions

1. What is the difference between the "kingdom of this world" and the "kingdom of God"?

_____

_____

_____

_____

_____

_____

2. Jesus tells us in scripture that the kingdom of God last forever; what is your understanding of eternity (forever)?

_____

_____

_____

_____

_____

_____

HALFTIME

St. Thomas More

Hall of Fame profile: St. Thomas More

Thomas More was an unlikely saint. He was Henry VIII's Lord Chancellor—a job that required dealing with the increasingly batty king's whims on a daily basis. More was a master at it, keeping the kingdom running smoothly while still managing to keep the king happy.

As a literary figure, More was famous for his satirical novel *Utopia,* in which he described an imaginary country where everything was run the way Thomas More would want it to be run.

In his own day, he was probably even more famous for his correspondence with Martin Luther, in which both men enthusiastically hurled obscenities at each other.

More enjoyed life. He had a sharp sense of humor, and he was famous for his wisecracks about the politics of the day. He liked the comforts money and position could bring him.

But he wouldn't compromise on his religion.

He certainly never wanted to be a martyr. But sometimes, if you take your faith seriously, life doesn't give you a choice.

When Henry VIII wanted to divorce his wife and the Pope wouldn't let him, the king threw a tantrum and declared himself head of the Church of England.

More couldn't go along with that. As King of England, Henry legitimately had the right to make the laws for his subjects. But Christ, not Henry, made the rules in the Church.

It came down to a battle between two kingdoms. Would More pick the kingdom of Christ, or the kingdom of Henry?

That was no contest, as far as More was concerned. To the last, he looked for some way to compromise—to satisfy the king without giving up his principles.

But the king wouldn't be satisfied. More loved his comfortable life, but he loved Christ more. He couldn't deny his real Lord.

So Thomas More was beheaded in 1535. On his way up the scaffold, he told one of the officials, "I pray you, Mr. Lieutenant, see me safe up. As for my coming down, I can shift for myself."

1. We don't think of Jesus as a king, and we definitely don't think of Him as a warrior.

2. But that's part of His nature; He came to make war on the devil.

3. We see images of Jesus as wimpy and passive, not very manly. It turns a lot of guys off to the practice of the faith.

4. Jesus was tough. One of His most challenging moments was in the Garden of Gethsemane (John 18), where He was sweating blood, beaten down by our sins. Six hundred soldiers come to arrest Him—strong, brutal men with weapons who would eventually torture Him. When Jesus said, "I am he," He knocked six hundred tough soldiers to the ground.

5. Jesus is no wimp. This is a warrior God who calls men to get up off their chairs and get serious about building the kingdom. When are you really going to stand up as a man?

6. It has to start with me and my family. What are people going to say about me? I don't care!

7. Thomas More: For the sake of our friendship, would you join me in hell?

8. No compromises. Every man has to be a king in his own home and say, "We've got to live differently."

9. The saints understood they were cooperating with God's grace to establish the kingdom in their hearts.

10. For a long time, it was easy and good for business to be in the Church. Everybody supported it. Now, it's countercultural. When it starts to cost something, many of us abandon the Church.

11. Many university campuses are openly hostile to Christianity. Those people will graduate and spread all over the culture. We have to wake up: now is the time.

12. It's "triumph of the Cross," not "triumph of the pillow." It's going to be hard.

13. Imagine you make it to heaven, and you look down and see your brother or your family saying, "Why didn't you tell me?" What about your grandchildren and great-grandchildren?

14. Have I left a Christ-shaped imprint in my children's lives? We could have a spectacular impact.

15. We're losing the battle of the kingdom by forfeit. We're just not showing up.

16. "The gates of hell" (or "powers of death" in some versions) "will not prevail against us" (Mt. 16). "Prevail" means "withstand." If we're active, the gates of hell will fall. The war has been won for us.

17. If we're passive, the principalities and powers will come rushing in.

18. Pornography is one of the ways the devil comes rushing in.

19. John 16:33: The war is over; the victory belongs to the Lord!

20. We're going to have battles, but don't give up. If you're down in the fourth quarter, you can't win on defense.

21. God has the power to get us out of this.

22. Are we afraid of a challenge? Where are our guts? Religion is an adventure. If you find it boring, you're not living the battle. It's boring because you're asleep.

23. People say the Church is full of hypocrites. But the Church is not a museum of saints. It's a hospital for sinners.

24. Working together to bring the whole world under Jesus Christ—that's what it means to be a Catholic.

25. It all starts right in our hearts. We're tempted to take the wrong side. We have to sacrifice our animal desires on the altar every day.

Knocking Roman
soldiers to the ground

So Judas, procuring a band of soldiers and some officers from the chief priests and the Pharisees, went there with lanterns and torches and weapons.

Then Jesus, knowing all that was to befall him, came forward and said to them, "Whom do you seek?"

They answered him, "Jesus of Nazareth."

Jesus said to them, "I am he." Judas, who betrayed him, was standing with them. When he said to them, "I am he," they drew back and fell to the ground.

(John 18:3–6)

Who do you say that I am?

Now when Jesus came into the district of Caesarea Philippi, he asked his disciples, "Who do men say that the Son of man is?"

And they said, "Some say John the Baptist, others say Elijah, and others Jeremiah or one of the prophets."

He said to them, "But who do you say that I am?"

Simon Peter replied, "You are the Christ, the Son of the living God."

And Jesus answered him, "Blessed are you, Simon Bar-Jona! For flesh and blood has not revealed this to you, but my Father who is in heaven. And I tell you, you are Peter, and on this rock I will build my Church, and the gates of Hades shall not prevail against it. I will give you the keys of the kingdom of heaven, and whatever you bind on earth shall be bound in heaven, and whatever you loose on earth shall be loosed in heaven."

(Matthew 16:13–19)

TIME OUT

<u>Warm-up questions</u>

1. What particular point(s) caught your attention the most in this segment?

_____

_____

_____

_____

_____

_____

_____

2. What is something useful that you learned from viewing this segment that you can apply in your own life?

_____

_____

_____

_____

_____

_____

_____

Workout questions

1. What does it mean to "Plant the flag of the kingdom of Christ in our hearts?"

_____

_____

_____

_____

_____

_____

_____

2. What are some of the obstacles in our lives that are preventing us from following the "Kingdom of God?"

_____

_____

_____

_____

_____

_____

_____

3. John the Baptist came to prepare the people to receive the kingdom of God; identify one way you can bring the kingdom of God into your home and into your workplace.

_____

_____

_____

_____

_____

_____

4. Name one area in your life that you have difficulty surrendering to the Lordship of Jesus.

_____

_____

_____

_____

_____

_____

_____

With Jesus, you have the power to win the battle.

➤ Jesus has won the war. But there are still battles and skirmishes.

➤ If you give your life to Christ, there's a power in you that's greater than any force that comes against you.

➤ The King Himself is alive in you, calling you to submit your heart to Him so He can lead you to freedom.

Be a man of action.

➤ Matthew 7:21: "Not every one who says to me, 'Lord, Lord,' shall enter the kingdom of heaven, but he who does the will of my Father who is in heaven."

➤ We were made to be men of action.

➤ Awaken the warrior inside.

➤ The world is waiting for us to join the victorious battle.

➤ We take "Thy kingdom come" for granted.

➤ There's only one chance.

➤ The choice is yours: heaven or hell?

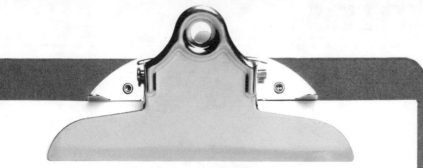

2 Minute Drill:
Personal Fitness Action Plan

Write out an action plan—I commit to becoming spiritually fit by...

NOTES

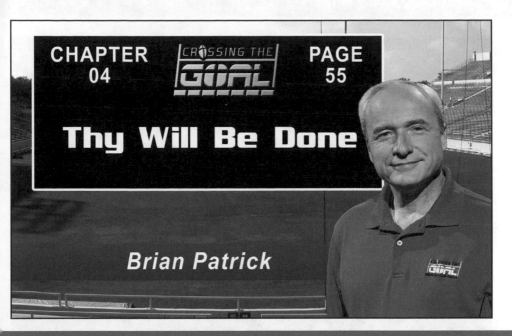

Thy Will Be Done

Brian Patrick

PRE-GAME

It's just four words in English: "Thy will be done." But those are four of the hardest words we'll ever pray—if we really mean them.

What we want, of course, is for *our* will to be done. Usually that's what we're praying for when we pray: "God, take away this pain, heal my friend with cancer, help me get through this math test."

Those are all good things to pray for. But we have to remember that God knows a little more than we do. Sometimes the things we think are best for us aren't what God knows is best for us. When that's true, we have to trust that God's will is better—even when it really hurts.

Jesus Himself knows better than anyone else how hard it is to pray these words. In Gethsemane, He prayed three times that He might avoid what He knew was coming. He prayed so long and hard that His disciples fell asleep waiting for Him. But He also had the faith to pray, "thy will be done":

> Then Jesus went with them to a place called Gethsemane, and he said to his disciples, "Sit here, while I go over there and pray." And taking with him Peter and the two sons of Zebedee, he began to be sorrowful and troubled.
>
> Then he said to them, "My soul is very sorrowful, even to death; remain here, and watch with me."
>
> And going a little farther he fell on his face and prayed, "My Father, if it be possible, let this chalice pass from me; nevertheless, not as I will, but as thou will."

> And he came to the disciples and found them sleeping; and he said to Peter, "So, could you not watch with me one hour? Watch and pray that you may not enter into temptation; the spirit indeed is willing, but the flesh is weak."
>
> Again, for the second time, he went away and prayed, "My Father, if this cannot pass unless I drink it, your will be done."
>
> And again he came and found them sleeping, for their eyes were heavy. So, leaving them again, he went away and prayed for the third time, saying the same words.
>
> Then he came to the disciples and said to them, "Are you still sleeping and taking your rest? Behold, the hour is at hand, and the Son of man is betrayed into the hands of sinners. Rise, let us be going; see, my betrayer is at hand."
>
> While he was still speaking, Judas came, one of the Twelve, and with him a great crowd with swords and clubs, from the chief priests and the elders of the people.
>
> (Matthew 26:36–47)

The crowd was coming to take Jesus away to be tortured and then crucified. Jesus knew they were coming. Nevertheless, that was the Father's will.

Do we have the faith to pray "thy will be done"? It's not always going to be easy. Sometimes God's will really hurts, because there's no way to accomplish it without pain.

But we know that God's will is best for us in the end.

KICKOFF

1. How do we know what God's will is?

2. Catechism 51–53: God desires that *all would be saved* and come to knowledge of the truth.

3. God's will is for every single human being to live with God forever in heaven.

4. God created us with a free will to choose life or death, right or wrong. Do we want to do His will or our will? Most of the time we choose our way. Hell is filled with "My ways."

5. Does God want us to go to church on Sunday? Of course, but that's not the main thing. He wants us to *want* to go to church on Sunday.

6. When we will what God wills, it brings joy to God's heart.

7. God, who is all-powerful, was willing to tolerate all the evil in the world to gain a greater good.

8. To do God's will, we have to bring our will into alignment with God's will. We have to give up what we will that's not consistent with God's will.

9. Jesus asks us to pray that we would have His passion for the salvation of souls.

10. That's why the Church is fundamentally missionary.

11. We want things our way.

12. It's one thing to stop sinning. That's good. But God wants us to share His passions—saving souls, healing injuries, serving the poor, bringing the Good News to people who haven't heard it. Then God's will is being done on earth as it is in heaven.

13. God wants to get us to church on Sunday, but then He wants to send us out the door to do His will.

God wants us all to be saved (Catechism 51-53)

51 "It pleased God, in his goodness and wisdom, to reveal himself and to make known the mystery of his will. His will was that men should have access to the Father, through Christ, the Word made flesh, in the Holy Spirit, and thus become sharers in the divine nature." (*Dei Verbum* 2; cf. Eph 1:9; 2:18; 2 Pet 1:4.)

52 God, who "dwells in unapproachable light," wants to communicate his own divine life to the men he freely created, in order to adopt them as his sons in his only-begotten Son (1 Tim 6:16, cf. Eph 1:4–5). By revealing himself God wishes to make them capable of responding to him, and of knowing him, and of loving him far beyond their own natural capacity.

53 The divine plan of Revelation is realized simultaneously "by deeds and words which are intrinsically bound up with each other" (Dei Verbum 2) and shed light on each another. It involves a specific divine pedagogy: God communicates himself to man gradually. He prepares him to welcome by stages the supernatural Revelation that is to culminate in the person and mission of the incarnate Word, Jesus Christ.

St. Irenaeus of Lyons repeatedly speaks of this divine pedagogy using the image of God and man becoming accustomed to one another: The Word of God dwelt in man and became the Son of man in order to accustom man to perceive God and to accustom God to dwell in man, according to the Father's pleasure.

GAME PLAN

1. Jesus is modeling in His own life the thing He is asking us to pray for: yielding our will to His will.

2. Even Jesus struggled: "Let this cup pass."

3. As hard as it looked, what held Him there was knowing that the Father is utterly trustworthy, no matter what the circumstances looked like.

4. Jesus makes it possible for us to move from "*my* will be done" to "*thy* will be done." That's the way to salvation.

5. On the Cross He broke the power of sin over us.

6. He gave us a new heart, so that we now have the capacity to *want* the will of God.

7. The power of the devil and his angels has been broken, but the devil and his angels are liars. They're not going to let you know that. You're going to feel like the same old man.

8. 1 Thessalonians 4:3: God's will is that we should become holy—set apart, living differently, completely owned and possessed by God.

9. Abstain from sexual immorality.

10. God's not opposed to sex—He created it. But when we misuse sex, we're saying no to God, the Creator, and His design and purpose.

11. He wants us to enjoy it according to His own will—within marriage, open to life, we find a sharing or communion of persons who can live out that joy.

12. God is the God of pleasure. Psalms 16:11: "In your right hand are pleasures for evermore."

13. As we live the right way, we can come to the knowledge of God. Then we can be saved.

14. God wants to move us from lust—drawing someone to myself for plea-sure—to love—giving ourselves to someone, which leads to another whole level of pleasure.

15. The Holy Spirit moves in us to want what God wants.

16. Our culture makes it very difficult to do this.

17. We're hardwired for comfort. But we have to step out of our comfort zone and allow His will to be done.

18. The spirit of Christ gives us the power to turn away from "it's all about me" and toward "what can I do for you?"—to be the person who radiates Christ and meets people where they are.

19. Romans 8: Put to death the deeds of the body and you will live.

20. The Holy Spirit helps us through Scripture, sacraments, prayer, and sup-port to move toward fulfilling the will of God.

21. Galatians 5:19–24: The works of the flesh and the fruits of the Spirit.

22. We can repent. We can turn to the Lord and allow His will to be done in our lives.

GAME PLAN SUMMARY

- The way to salvation: move from "my will be done" to "thy will be done."
- Don't get caught up in sexual immorality.
- Step out of your comfort zone and allow God's will to be done.

God calls us to holiness

Finally, brethren, we beseech and exhort you in the Lord Jesus, that as you learned from us how you ought to walk and to please God, just as you are doing, you do so more and more. For you know what instructions we gave you through the Lord Jesus. For this is the will of God, your sanctification: that you abstain from immorality; that each one of you know how to control his own body in holiness and honor, not in the passion of lust like heathen who do not know God; that no man transgress, and wrong his brother in this matter, because the Lord is an avenger in all these things, as we solemnly forewarned you.

For God has not called us for uncleanness, but in holiness. Therefore whoever disregards this, disregards not man but God, who gives his Holy Spirit to you.

(1 Thessalonians 4:1–8)

Dead to sin, alive in righteousness

For those who live according to the flesh set their minds on the things of the flesh, but those who live according to the Spirit set their minds on the things of the Spirit. To set the mind on the flesh is death, but to set the mind on the Spirit is life and peace.

For the mind that is set on the flesh is hostile to God; it does not submit to God's law, indeed it cannot; and those who are in the flesh cannot please God. But you are not in the flesh, you are in the Spirit, if the Spirit of God really dwells in you. Any one who does not have the Spirit of Christ does not belong to him.

But if Christ is in you, although your bodies are dead because of sin, your spirits are alive because of righteousness. If the Spirit of him who raised Jesus from the dead dwells in you, he who raised Christ Jesus from the dead will give life to your mortal bodies also through his Spirit who dwells in you.

So then, brethren, we are debtors, not to the flesh, to live according to the flesh—for if you live according to the flesh you will die, but if by the Spirit you put to death the deeds of the body you will live.

(Romans 8:5–13)

60

TIME OUT

<u>Warm-up questions</u>

1. What particular point(s) caught your attention the most in this segment?

_____

_____

_____

_____

_____

_____

_____

2. What is something useful that you learned from viewing this segment that you can apply in your own life?

_____

_____

_____

_____

_____

_____

_____

Workout questions

1. "Thy will be done" involves trusting the Lord more than ourselves. In what areas of your life do you have the most difficulty trusting the Lord?

_____

_____

_____

_____

_____

_____

2. It's hard to hear the Lord when we're surrounded by noise! What are your favorite places to go to and spend quiet time?

_____

_____

_____

_____

_____

_____

HALFTIME

Flesh or Spirit?

In his letter to the Galatians, St. Paul gives us a list of the works of the flesh and the fruit of the Spirit. His lists are long paragraphs, but that's because St. Paul didn't have PowerPoint. Let's pretend he was a modern-day, motivational speaker. He would have given us bulleted lists to make them easy to read. And once we saw those lists, it would be clear to us instantly whether God's will was really being done in our lives.

But I say, walk by the Spirit, and do not gratify the desires of the flesh. For the desires of the flesh are against the Spirit, and the desires of the Spirit are against the flesh; for these are opposed to each other, to prevent you from doing what you would. But if you are led by the Spirit you are not under the law.

Now the works of the flesh are plain:

- fornication
- impurity
- licentiousness
- idolatry
- sorcery

- enmity
- strife
- jealousy
- anger
- selfishness

- dissension
- party spirit
- envy
- drunkenness
- carousing

and the like. I warn you, as I warned you before, that those who do such things shall not inherit the kingdom of God.

But the fruit of the Spirit is

- love
- joy
- peace

- patience
- kindness
- goodness

- faithfulness
- gentleness
- self-control

against such there is no law.

And those who belong to Christ Jesus have crucified the flesh with its passions and desires. If we live by the Spirit, let us also walk by the Spirit.

(Galatians 5:16–25)

RED ZONE // RED ZONE

1. Put your trust and faith in God.

2. The Lord can change our way of living when we decide to go *His* way.

3. *Crossing the Goal* came about through prayer. Long before we think about what God wants, God is already preparing us.

4. Many of us are on the sidelines. Take it to prayer. Were you affected by abortion, pornography? Find your wounded portion in our culture, and then with God's grace go to war.

5. How do I know what He wants me to do?

6. Put yourself in a position to hear God speak. Use the human element.

RED ZONE // RED ZONE

7. The final decision happens in the heart. Seek God's will for you.

8. Men are afraid to change.

9. One thing we know for sure: we know when we're *not* doing God's will. Not doing the things we know are *not* God's will is a good place to start.

10. Why does the Catholic Church exist? To evangelize, to communicate the truth.

11. There aren't many men doing evangelization. Look in the mirror. It's us. We have to spread the Good News.

12. Change yourself. Once you change, your family changes. One of the best places to start evangelizing is your own home.

13. Christian businessmen can use their businesses to bring the truth to people. You can still make money and get ahead.

14. Businessmen put all kinds of money into their businesses. Evangelization struggles—but we have the greatest thing in the world to sell: Jesus Christ.

15. Until our hearts fall in love with Christ, we're not going to have that passion.

16. Cultivate an eternal perspective. Nobody cares in heaven that you drove a Ferrari. In heaven, they'll ask, "Did you bring anybody with you?"

17. Lots of people worry about people who never hear the Gospel. But the bigger question is whether we will be saved if we don't evangelize.

18. Someone has to tell them, and it has to be us.

19. You can't share the Good News if you don't have it.

20. You can share it one-on-one. You don't have to tell the whole world at once—it's just one beggar telling another beggar where the feast is.

21. Small groups are good: that's how you learn and grow, mentored by other guys.

22. When you're on fire for the Lord, people will see it in your eyes.

TIME OUT

Warm-up questions

1. What particular point(s) caught your attention the most in this segment?

_____

_____

_____

_____

_____

_____

_____

2. What is something useful that you learned from viewing this segment that you can apply in your own life?

_____

_____

_____

_____

_____

_____

_____

Workout questions

1. Throughout history, the saints have listened and followed the will of God. Share a favorite story of when a saint followed the will of God.

_____

_____

_____

_____

_____

_____

2. Think back to a time that God's will was obvious in your life? Share this story with your brothers.

_____

_____

_____

_____

_____

_____

3. What needs "fixing" in your community? Abortion centers? Porn shops? How can you and your group work to fix these problems?

_____

_____

_____

_____

_____

_____

4. Who in your family needs most to hear the Good News? What can you do to share God's love with them?

_____

_____

_____

_____

_____

_____

_____

What are you doing with your time, money, and abilities?

➤ Go get your credit card or bank statement.

➤ Where are you spending your money?

➤ How much of it is for God's kingdom?

Step into the culture with the light God gives you.

➤ The world is desperately waiting for us to catch fire.

➤ What part of culture most disappoints you, drives you crazy?

➤ God placed that frustration in your heart to lead you on an adventure of changing the world.

➤ When you place yourself on the front lines, God will be in overdrive, making you the man you're supposed to be.

➤ None of us are worthy.

➤ But a sinner can do it.

➤ Follow Jesus' way.

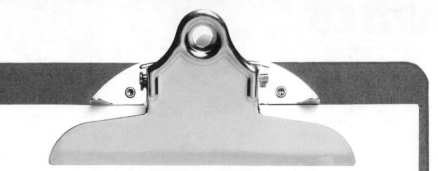

2 Minute Drill:
Personal Fitness Action Plan

Write out an action plan—I commit to becoming spiritually fit by...

NOTES

Our Daily Bread

Brian Patrick

PRE-GAME

Where will the money come from?

How many times have you heard yourself asking that? Especially when money is tight, it's really hard to trust that God will provide what we need.

And we're not supposed to be lazy. We need to work for a living. "For even when we were with you, we gave you this command," St. Paul told the Thessalonians: "If any one will not work, let him not eat" (2 Thessalonians 3:10).

But when we're doing our best, we have to trust that God will give us what we need. And we have to use what we have to do God's will, confident that God will still provide.

Francis of Assisi was an ordinary young man who liked cool clothes and rock stars—or at least the nearest medieval equivalent, which was French minstrels. And his father was a rich merchant, so he could afford the luxuries he enjoyed.

But one day, while he was in town to sell a load of expensive luxury fabrics for the family business, a beggar came up to him and asked for some money. Francis didn't give him anything, but he couldn't forget that beggar. When he sold the fabric, he ran after the beggar and gave him all the money he'd made from the sale.

Francis' father was furious. What kind of way is that to run a business?

But Francis was learning something his father would never understand. Doing the Lord's work is more important than making money. And when you're doing the Lord's work, the Lord takes care of you.

Later on, of course, St. Francis of Assisi founded the Franciscan Order, a group of Christians dedicated to doing God's work in poverty. Embracing the poor life, they lived on what people gave them from day to day, not caring about tomorrow. That freed them from that burning question, "Where will the money come from?"

Of course, they couldn't have cool clothes and rock concerts all the time anymore. But Francis found he was much happier without those things. When he trusted in God to provide, he could concentrate on the things that were really worthwhile.

KICKOFF

1. It's hard for us to learn dependence.

2. Do we really believe God will provide for our *needs,* or are we worried that God won't give us what we *want?*

3. Matthew 6: Don't be anxious about what you're going to eat, drink, or wear.

4. Is Jesus asking us to do something literally impossible?

5. Jesus tells us: The devil has been telling lies about our Father. God will provide for us, and He wants us to rely on Him, because there will be times when your trust will be tested.

6. Why isn't God answering my prayer? Sometimes the answer is *no,* or *not yet.*

7. A year and a half later, you may be thankful you didn't get what you asked for. God knows what you don't.

8. Jesus says that *unbelievers* are worried about their daily needs all the time. But you know that your Father in heaven knows what you need.

9. We say, "Give us *this* day our daily bread," not "Give us our bread for seventeen years from now."

10. God wants to meet us where we are every day. He won't make provision for us ten years from now.

"No one can serve two masters; for either he will hate the one and love the other, or he will be devoted to the one and despise the other. You cannot serve God and mammon.

"Therefore I tell you, do not be anxious about your life, what you shall eat or what you shall drink, nor about your body, what you shall put on. Is not life more than food, and the body more than clothing? Look at the birds of the air: they neither sow nor reap nor gather into barns, and yet your heavenly Father feeds them. Are you not of more value than they? And which of you by being anxious can add one cubit to his span of life? And why are you anxious about clothing? Consider the lilies of the field, how they grow; they neither toil nor spin; yet I tell you, even Solomon in all his glory was not clothed like one of these. But if God so clothes the grass of the field, which today is alive and tomorrow is thrown into the oven, will he not much more clothe you, O you of little faith? Therefore do not be anxious, saying, 'What shall we eat?' or 'What shall we drink?' or 'What shall we wear?' For the Gentiles seek all these things; and your heavenly Father knows that you need them all. But seek first his kingdom and his righteousness, and all these things shall be yours as well.

"Therefore do not be anxious about tomorrow, for tomorrow will be anxious for itself. Let the day's own trouble be sufficient for the day."

(Matthew 6:24–34)

GAME PLAN

1. The image of "daily bread" goes back to the manna from heaven in Exodus.

2. The people were told to gather what they needed and no more. If they gathered too much, it rotted.

3. God wanted to give them just enough for the day. He was training Israel to look to Him for their provision.

4. This isn't an exhortation to idleness. We're supposed to work as hard as we can at what we're called to do, but God will provide for us through and beyond that.

5. We're tempted to trust in money. Scripture talks about money more than almost anything else. Money isn't wrong, but we rely on money instead of God.

6.   Why does our money say "In God we trust"? To remind us to put our real trust in God, not in money.

7.   When we don't trust God, we become anxious.

8.   Money is part of what God gives us.

9.   Inside-trader tip: Put your treasure in heaven. It's an investment that will really last. If your treasure is in heaven, your heart will follow.

10.   Take what you need for yourself, and invest the rest in the work of the Lord.

11.   We're instructed to give back a *tithe*—the tenth part of what we earn.

12.   We need to trust God and remember that it's *all* his. As a symbolic gesture, we give Him the first fruits back. Then we use what we need and invest the rest in human lives.

13.   Proverbs 30:8: "Feed me with the food that is needful for me." If I have too much, I get lazy in my spiritual life and forget about God. But if I live in moderation, investing the rest in others, I'm fulfilling God's will.

14.   Scripture teaches us how to have the right relationship to money. It belongs to Him. I'm the Lord's money manager; the money's not mine.

15.   We can look at it that way because we know the Lord is our portion. The Lord will take care of us.

16.   "Taste and see that the Lord is good."

17.   Our money is the Lord's because *we* are the Lord's. Everything we have is His already.

18.   "Render unto Caesar what is Caesar's." How do you know it's Caesar's? It has Caesar's image on it. "Render unto God what is God's." What bears God's image? We do.

GAME PLAN SUMMARY

- Work as hard as you can, but trust God to provide.
- Put your treasure in heaven, and your heart will follow.
- Remember that you're God's money manager. It doesn't really belong to you.

Render unto Caesar

The Pharisees loved to set little traps for Jesus. This was one of their best: is it lawful to pay taxes to Caesar? If He said yes, they could call Him a collaborator with the evil Roman occupation. If He said no, they could report Him to the Romans as a traitor. But Jesus, as usual, used their trap to teach us something universal about our relationship with God.

And they sent to him some of the Pharisees and some of the Herodians, to entrap him in his talk. And they came and said to him, "Teacher, we know that you are true, and care for no man; for you do not regard the position of men, but truly teach the way of God. Is it lawful to pay taxes to Caesar, or not? Should we pay them, or should we not?"

But knowing their hypocrisy, he said to them, "Why put me to the test? Bring me a coin, and let me look at it."

And they brought one.

And he said to them, "Whose likeness and inscription is this?"

They said to him, "Caesar's."

Jesus said to them, "Render to Caesar the things that are Caesar's, and to God the things that are God's." And they were amazed at him.

(Mark 12:13–17)

TIME OUT

Warm-up questions

1. What particular point(s) caught your attention the most in this segment?

_____

_____

_____

_____

_____

_____

_____

2. What is something useful that you learned from viewing this segment that you can apply in your own life?

_____

_____

_____

_____

_____

_____

_____

Workout questions

1. What new insights did you gain about the Christian approach to money?

_____

_____

_____

_____

_____

_____

_____

2. How would you react to God if you lost your job or 50% of your retirement fund tomorrow?

_____

_____

_____

_____

_____

_____

HALFTIME

Manna from heaven

When the people of Israel grumbled that they had nothing to eat in the desert, God provided their daily bread—"a fine, flake-like thing, fine as hoarfrost on the ground." When they asked, "What is it?"—in Hebrew, "manna"—Moses told them it was the bread the Lord had given them.

> And the LORD said to Moses, "I have heard the murmurings of the sons of Israel; say to them, 'At twilight you shall eat flesh, and in the morning you shall be filled with bread; then you shall know that I am the LORD your God.'"

In the evening quails came up and covered the camp; and in the morning dew lay round about the camp. And when the dew had gone up, there was on the face of the wilderness a fine, flake-like thing, fine as hoarfrost on the ground.

When the people of Israel saw it, they said to one another, "What is it?" For they did not know what it was.

And Moses said to them, "It is the bread which the LORD has given you to eat. This is what the LORD has commanded: 'Gather of it, every man of you, as much as he can eat; you shall take an omer apiece, according to the number of the persons whom each of you has in his tent.'"

And the sons of Israel did so; they gathered, some more, some less. But when they measured it with an omer, he that gathered much had nothing over, and he that gathered little had no lack; each gathered according to what he could eat.

And Moses said to them, "Let no man leave any of it till the morning."

But they did not listen to Moses; some left part of it till the morning, and it bred worms and became foul; and Moses was angry with them.

(Exodus 16:11–20)

RED ZONE // RED ZON

1. Curtis' story: He went back to graduate school, ran out of money, and ran out of food. As he was praying, a neighbor knocked on the door with extra spaghetti. God'll let us sweat, but He never lets us down.

2. Danny's story: Through drinking, he lost a fortune, even his house. After he prayed, a new job came through. The Lord will provide; the Father knows your needs.

3. Many of us have lost jobs. That's big stuff. But there's a learning curve. Paul says, "I have learned the secret of contentment. I've gone hungry, I've been abased, and what I discovered was that even when I don't have what I think I need, God provides for me."

RED ZONE // RED ZON

4. It happens in God's time frame, not ours. God may let us get down to the wire because He wants us to see where the provision comes from.

5. God blesses us because He wants us to pray to Him. When He does bless us, we turn away. When He withholds the blessings temporarily, we're back praying.

6. Then He shows us that when we turn to Him, He cares for us.

7. Sometimes when we panic, we accuse God.

8. The Lord has to teach us that He is trustworthy. He takes us to the limit and then provides for us.

9. Throughout history, we see God leading us to places where we *have* to trust Him.

10. Moses leads the people out of Egypt, and God's plan is to lead them to a giant sea with no bridge. Not a good plan. And then the Egyptian army starts to attack. And then the sea parts.

11. Jesus Himself lay in the tomb for three days—but on the third day He came back.

12. The greatest gift God has given us—His daily bread—is the Eucharist.

13. We take the Eucharist for granted. We have the opportunity to attend Mass daily. Just one extra day a week will help connect you spiritually to our Lord.

14. The Catechism says the bread of life—our daily bread—is word and sacrament. If you can't get to Mass every day, you need to be in the Word of God every day.

15. Our mind is like a sponge. If you throw it in muddy water, it comes out full of mud.

16. God's Word is like fresh water that washes over our mind cleansing and purifying our thoughts and the habit patterns of our mind.

17. You get out of it what you put into it. If you really believe that Jesus gave Himself to us body, blood, soul and divinity, why wouldn't you want to go to Mass as often as you can?

TIME OUT

Warm-up questions

1. What particular point(s) caught your attention the most in this segment?

_____

_____

_____

_____

_____

_____

2. What is something useful that you learned from viewing this segment that you can apply in your own life?

_____

_____

_____

_____

_____

_____

_____

Workout questions

1. How much money or how many material goods do you need to be content? Have you reached that place of contentment?

_____

_____

_____

_____

_____

_____

_____

2. Share an experience of how God provided for you or your family.

_____

_____

_____

_____

_____

_____

3. Share an experience when God led you to a place where you had to grow and trust in Him.

_____

_____

_____

_____

_____

_____

4. Do you tithe? If so, share how God led you to do that. If not, why should you consider starting that discipline?

_____

_____

_____

_____

_____

_____

_____

Seek first the Kingdom of God.

➤ In the face of crisis, Jesus leads us to make a decision.

➤ If you're in the midst of panic, seek first the kingdom of God.

Making time for God every day.

➤ As we seek, then the things will be added on.

➤ God wants to be first in our lives.

➤ Open up the Gospels and spend some time with our Lord.

➤ Get to Mass one more time a week.

COACHING POINT

Don't treat God like He's Monty Hall

➤ Don't cut deals with the Lord.

➤ Trust that God will supply your daily needs.

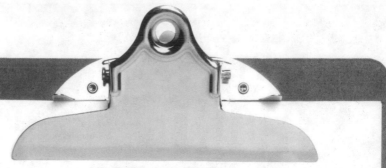

2 Minute Drill:
Personal Fitness Action Plan

Write out an action plan—I commit to becoming spiritually fit by…

NOTES

Forgive Us Our Trespasses

Brian Patrick

PRE-GAME

We're going to let Jesus Himself tell us a pre-game story today, because we know Jesus tells good stories, and because we're going to keep coming back to this story throughout the session.

The story begins, as many of Jesus' stories do, when one of the disciples asked Him a question: how many times should we forgive?

Peter must have thought he was being pretty generous. Seven times—that's a whole lot of forgiving. Imagine! Your friend betrays you *seven times,* and you still forgive him!

But Peter still doesn't get it, Jesus says.

> Then Peter came up and said to him, "Lord, how often shall my brother sin against me, and I forgive him? As many as seven times?"
>
> Jesus said to him, "I do not say to you seven times, but seventy times seven.
>
> "Therefore the kingdom of heaven may be compared to a king who wished to settle accounts with his servants. When he began the reckoning, one was brought to him who owed him ten thousand talents; and as he could not pay, his lord ordered him to be sold, with his wife and children and all that he had, and payment to be made. So the servant fell on his knees, imploring him, 'Lord, have patience with me, and I will pay you everything.' And out of pity for him the lord of that servant released him and forgave him the debt.

> "But that same servant, as he went out, came upon one of his fellow servants who owed him a hundred denarii; and seizing him by the throat he said, 'Pay what you owe.'
>
> "So his fellow servant fell down and pleaded with him, 'Have patience with me, and I will pay you.'
>
> "He refused and went and put him in prison till he should pay the debt.
>
> "When his fellow servants saw what had taken place, they were greatly distressed, and they went and reported to their lord all that had taken place.
>
> "Then his lord summoned him and said to him, 'You wicked servant! I forgave you all that debt because you pleaded with me; and should not you have had mercy on your fellow servant, as I had mercy on you?' And in anger his lord delivered him to the jailers, till he should pay all his debt.
>
> "So also my heavenly Father will do to every one of you, if you do not forgive your brother from your heart."
>
> (Matthew 18:21–35)

This man had an enormous debt—millions and millions of dollars by today's standards. He couldn't pay it, and the law allowed his creditor to sell him and his whole family as slaves.

But the creditor didn't. He forgave the debt—not because he had to, but simply because the man asked.

The forgiveness wasn't unconditional, however. The creditor expected that his debtor would also be forgiving.

And that's the perspective we have to keep in mind.

What God has forgiven us is a debt so enormous that we can never repay it. But He expects something in return. He expects that we'll be forgiving, too. As Jesus Himself has told us, we'll be measured with our own stick (Matthew 7:2).

KICKOFF

1. "As we"—two very important words.

2. If you expect to be forgiven, you have to forgive. If you don't show mercy, you won't get mercy. The measure with which you measure out will be measured against you.

3. It's easier said than done.

4. There will be times when dear friends will betray you. You still need to forgive.

5. Jesus will say, "How many times did you ask me to forgive you as you forgave others?" That's going to be the measure.

6. The prayer is almost a curse that we put on ourselves.

7. It's hard to forgive. But we can do it with the Lord's help.

8. If it's a big wound, we have to work through it, because it keeps coming back.

GAME PLAN

1. Forgiveness is the heart of God, the foundation of the whole Christian life.

2. Everything about God's heart is revealed in the person of Jesus Christ on the Cross: "Father, forgive them, for they don't know what they're doing." They're trapped in cycles of sin, revenge, self-protection—all the stuff that separates us from God and one another.

3. The thing that breaks it is forgiveness.

4. Matthew 18: The man forgiven a huge debt can't forgive his neighbor. We are completely in debt to God. God wants to give us mercy—and then says, "Now that I've given it to you, give it to others."

5. Jesus is really serious about this. If you don't forgive, don't expect to go to heaven. Forgiveness is the foundation of our relationship.

6. The Apostles asked, "How many times do I have to forgive somebody?" "Seventy times seven"—a perfect number meaning there's no limit.

7. Unforgiveness blocks the advancement of God's kingdom. We pray, "Thy will be done." Forgiveness is God's will.

8. We're charged to extend mercy and forgiveness wherever we go to extend peace, because we've been given a superabundance of mercy.

9. Unforgiveness dams up the flow of the Holy Spirit. Forgiveness breaks it open.

10. What is the biggest obstacle to people working together? Unforgiveness. Unforgiveness creates bitterness in us, and we can't receive God's love.

11. How do you forgive serious wounds?

12. Don't say "No big deal." It is a big deal. It *did* hurt, but I appreciate your taking the time to ask for forgiveness, and I forgive you. That's dealing with the issue.

13. We shouldn't be surprised when we wound one another. We are broken people. If we spend time together, one of us will do something that hurts the other one. We'll need forgiveness to keep our relationship.

14. They will know we are Christians by our love.

15. If we're not willing to work through forgiveness, we're actually blocking the witness to who Christ is.

16. Guys think forgiveness or asking for forgiveness is weak or wimpy. We have to get over that.

GAME PLAN SUMMARY

- Break the cycle of sin with forgiveness.
- Acknowledge the hurt—but forgive anyway.
- Use your forgiveness to show the world who Christ is.

TIME OUT

Warm-up questions

1. What particular point(s) caught your attention the most in this segment?

_____

_____

_____

_____

_____

_____

_____

2. What is something useful that you learned from viewing this segment that you can apply in your own life?

_____

_____

_____

_____

_____

_____

_____

Workout questions

3. Who do you relate more to in the Gospel story: the unforgiving servant or the lord who is angry over someone else's unforgiveness? Why?

_____

_____

_____

_____

_____

_____

4. How does having trust in Jesus help us to forgive those who have hurt us?

_____

_____

_____

_____

_____

_____

_____

HALFTIME

Measured with your own ruler

Why is forgiveness so important?

Because we all need it. Not one of us is perfect, and most of us are a good bit less perfect than we think.

A while ago, there was a scientific study in the news. Researchers asked participants to perform a certain task, and rated how well they did that. Then they asked the participants themselves to rate their own performance.

The result was not terribly surprising: the worse the subjects' performance, the more likely they were to think they were doing a good job.

It's easy to laugh at that. Think of all the people we see every day who think they're good at what they do, but are really miserable incompetents. Think of all the people we see who think they're good, but are really miserable sinners.

But does it ever occur to us that we might be one of those people?

This is what Jesus is warning us about. We think we can see other people's faults very clearly. But we can't really see clearly at all, because our own faults blind us.

So He gives us a stern warning. Be careful how you judge other people, because you'll be measured with your own ruler.

> Judge not, that you be not judged. For with the judgment you pronounce you will be judged, and the measure you give will be the measure you get.
>
> Why do you see the speck that is in your brother's eye, but do not notice the log that is in your own eye? Or how can you say to your brother, 'Let me take the speck out of your eye,' when there is the log in your own eye? You hypocrite, first take the log out of your own eye, and then you will see clearly to take the speck out of your brother's eye.
>
> (Matthew 7:1–5)

1. Unforgiveness can eat you alive inside. It leads to anger and resentment.

2. Danny's story: Lured into a shaky investment by a friend he trusted, he lost thousands. He wanted to get back at his friend. But he suffered so much with the anger that he knew he had to forgive him. When he did, the relationship was restored.

3. It was a *decision* to forgive.

4. The devil is tricky—he keeps bringing up the things that make you angry. Unforgiveness is like a slow-motion replay of our pain and anger.

5. It's a profoundly human experience. St. Paul and St. Barnabas were separated for years because they couldn't work together. Our Lord was betrayed by Judas, a trusted friend.

6. Peter's experience: He's sure his wife is wrong and stubbornly gives her the silent treatment for a day or two. The Lord is saying, "Why are you stopping up my grace? How many times do I have to tell you?"

7. Sometimes you have to take the initiative in forgiveness.

8. "Blessed are the merciful, for they shall obtain mercy" (Matthew 5:7). We need mercy. We get it by showing it to others.

9. Forgiveness is a powerful key for unlocking God's mercy.

10. Some situations are so tough that you don't know how to forgive. Bring it to the Lord in prayer. Say, "Lord, I'm powerless. I hate that guy. I want to hurt that guy. It scares me. Please help me."

11. It's a decision to yield ourselves to the Lord's will. He will give us the grace we need to overcome our hatred.

12. Many times unforgiveness is passed through the family for years.

13. You have to let it go today. Don't let the sun set on your anger.

14. When you want revenge, remember that the measure you measured out is coming back against you.

15. Just say, "I yield my rights, Lord. I want to go your way. I really don't want to get the judgment I deserve!"

16. Even if the person you forgive is unrepentant, God's justice will be more than adequate to take care of it.

RED ZONE // RED ZONE

TIME OUT

Warm-up questions

1. What particular point(s) caught your attention the most in this segment?

_____

_____

_____

_____

_____

_____

_____

2. What is something useful that you learned from viewing this segment that you can apply in your own life?

_____

_____

_____

_____

_____

_____

_____

Workout questions

1. What should the attitude of our hearts be towards those who have hurt us? On the same question, what should the attitude of our hearts be towards those we have hurt?

_____

_____

_____

_____

_____

_____

_____

2. Do you forgive others as Christ forgives you? What makes this great command of the Lord's so difficult for us?

_____

_____

_____

_____

_____

_____

_____

3. Is it possible to truly say that you love God if you are carrying a huge burden of anger and unforgiveness?

_____

_____

_____

_____

_____

_____

_____

4. Who in your life has shown you what true forgiveness is? How did they do that?

_____

_____

_____

_____

_____

_____

_____

Is there someone you need to forgive?

➤ Or someone you need to ask forgiveness of?

➤ Ask the Lord for strength.

➤ Make the decision to move on the command of the Lord.

Be mindful of the impact you have on others.

➤ Are we making it hard on other people to forgive us?

➤ Can we be more attentive to the people around us?

➤ Make sure your impact is a Christ-shaped impact.

➤ When you point, you have one finger pointing at them and three back at yourself.

➤ Find someone, especially in your family, and ask forgiveness and give them forgiveness.

2 Minute Drill:
Personal Fitness Action Plan

Write out an action plan—I commit to becoming spiritually fit by...

NOTES

Lead Us Not Into Temptation

Brian Patrick

PRE-GAME

King David was the model for all the kings of Israel, the man after God's own heart, who built up the nation and led it in worshiping God. Yet he was also a sinner—with not just little sins, but great big horrible sins. Scripture tells us how he fell into temptation, and how that temptation led him on a downward spiral into the darkest crimes.

> In the spring of the year, the time when kings go forth to battle, David sent Joab, and his servants with him, and all Israel; and they ravaged the Ammonites, and besieged Rabbah. But David remained at Jerusalem.
>
> It happened, late one afternoon, when David arose from his couch and was walking upon the roof of the king's house, that he saw from the roof a woman bathing; and the woman was very beautiful. And David sent and inquired about the woman. And one said, "Is not this Bathsheba, the daughter of Eliam, the wife of Uriah the Hittite?"
>
> So David sent messengers, and took her; and she came to him, and he lay with her. (Now she was purifying herself from her uncleanness.) Then she returned to her house. And the woman conceived; and she sent and told David, "I am with child."
>
> (2 Samuel 11:1–5)

David tried to cover up his adultery by giving Uriah, one of his best soldiers, leave to go back home and be with his wife. That way he'd never know that the child wasn't his. But Uriah, good captain that he was, refused to go home while there was a battle on. No matter how hard David tried to persuade him, he wouldn't go home to his wife. Now David was desperate.

> In the morning David wrote a letter to Joab, and sent it by the hand of Uriah. In the letter he wrote, "Set Uriah in the forefront of the hardest fighting, and then draw back from him, that he may be struck down, and die." And as Joab was besieging the city, he assigned Uriah to the place where he knew there were valiant men. And the men of the city came out and fought with Joab; and some of the servants of David among the people fell. Uriah the Hittite was slain also.
> (2 Samuel 11:14–17)

Any one of us in his place could have seen what David saw from his rooftop, and we might have continued to look, and had some lusting in the heart to mention at confession. But David gave in to temptation. And that one sin led him, tragically, to the horrible crime of murder.

That's why temptation is such a big deal.

KICKOFF

1. Does God tempt us? Obviously not. James 1:13: God tempts no one.

2. Jesus is giving us a preemptive prayer.

3. We live in a constant spiritual battle. Jesus is leading us into a disposition of vigilance; we need to be alert.

4. We're going to encounter challenges. God will allow us to be tested— like teaching a child to ride a bike. The teacher has to let go of the bike, or the child will never learn to ride.

5. God wants to teach us how to walk spiritually. He'll allow us to go out into deep water, but we need to know ahead of time that He's not going to let us drown while we're out there.

6. Luke 4:1–13: The temptation of Jesus. The devil failed, but at the end he said, "I'll be back at a more opportune time." It's not *if,* but *when.*

7. But the Lord went out not by Himself, but with the Holy Spirit.

8. The devil waits for your weak moments, and then comes after you.

9. All he can do is tempt you, but if we say yes to the temptation, he wins in that particular instance.

10. We need to learn to fight with the weapons the Lord has given us.

11. Sometimes we allow the temptation to stay. Temptation feels good.

12. We need to recognize what it is, and call on God to help us. Then run. Get out of there.

God tempts no one

Let no one say when he is tempted, "I am tempted by God"; for God cannot be tempted with evil and he himself tempts no one; but each person is tempted when he is lured and enticed by his own desire. Then desire when it has conceived gives birth to sin; and sin when it is full-grown brings forth death.

(James 1:13–15)

GAME PLAN

1. We're to pray for the grace we need to stand against temptation.

2. The devil wants to lead us into temptation: to seduce us into doing something that's going to separate us from God.

3. James 1:14: Each person is tempted when he is enticed by his own desire.

4. We've been baptized and set free from our fallen nature, but we have a fallen nature: we're still tempted by our desire—lust, anger, revenge, avarice.

5. Temptation is not a sin. I can be tempted with all kinds of stuff, but if I keep resisting I haven't sinned.

6. But when I say yes to the temptation, it grows into sin.

7. Sin leads to death, because sin is denying God—saying, "I know you don't want me to, but I'm going to do it anyway." It breaks our relationship with God. If the sin is bad enough, it could literally kill us. That's what the devil wants: our spiritual death.

8. To avoid falling into temptation, lead a life committed to the Word of God. Begin to read the Scriptures.

9. Proverbs 1:33: "But he who listens to me will dwell secure and will be at ease, without dread of evil."

10. You can grow strong by listening to the Lord's Word in Scripture, then receiving the Eucharist. The Lord will deliver us from evil.

11. In our Baptism, He's given us the Holy Spirit.

12. Take up our weapons against sin, Paul says. Romans 6:12. Do not yield your members to sin, for sin will have no dominion over you.

13. By the death and resurrection of Jesus Christ, we've been given a new power to overcome temptation and sin.

14. We've been given freedom, but we still have weaknesses. Hebrews 12:4: You have not yet resisted to the point of shedding blood.

15. We really haven't tried that hard. Hebrews says, "Guys, come on—you can do more!"

16. You need a "no-limit" commitment to fighting sin at all costs, because sin is the only thing that ultimately can get us.

17. When we live that way, the *temptation* becomes a *test.* Instead of falling into sin, we grow in our sonship. We become the men we were meant to be.

18. One of the strategies of the devil is to confuse us about sin—it's not really a sin, it's not a big deal. We need to be very clear about what sin is.

19. Heart, soul, and mind must be set against sin.

GAME PLAN SUMMARY

- Read Scripture. Lead a life committed to the Word of God.
- Commit to fighting sin at all costs.
- Be very clear about what sin is, and set your heart, soul, and mind against it.

At ease from the dread of evil

For the simple are killed by their turning away, and the complacence of fools destroys them;

but he who listens to me will dwell secure and will be at ease, without dread of evil.

(Proverbs 1:32–33)

You haven't shed your blood yet

Consider him who endured from sinners such hostility against himself, so that you may not grow weary or fainthearted. In your struggle against sin you have not yet resisted to the point of shedding your blood.

(Hebrews 12:3–4)

TIME OUT

Warm-up questions

1. What particular point(s) caught your attention the most in this segment?

_____

_____

_____

_____

_____

_____

_____

2. What is something useful that you learned from viewing this segment that you can apply in your own life?

_____

_____

_____

_____

_____

_____

_____

Workout questions

1. David the prophet was tempted by a glance that led to sin. What are other devices (e.g., money) the devil uses to tempt us to fall into sin?

_____

_____

_____

_____

_____

_____

2. Listening to the news, we hear on a regular basis how prominent figures in our society fall prey to temptations. What is your reaction to that? Why?

_____

_____

_____

_____

_____

_____

HALFTIME

Dead to sin, alive in Christ

If you're dead, you can't sin anymore, St. Paul says. That's the good part of being dead.

Of course, there are disadvantages to being dead, too.

But St. Paul gives us some really amazing news: we can have the good parts of being dead without the bad parts. When we were baptized into Christ, we were baptized into His death. We died to sin. Now we have the grace to overcome sin and live forever with Christ.

Do you not know that all of us who have been baptized into Christ Jesus were baptized into his death? We were buried therefore with him by baptism into death, so that as Christ was raised from the dead by the glory of the Father, we too might walk in newness of life. For if we have been united with him in a death like his, we shall certainly be united with him in a resurrection like his.

We know that our former man was crucified with him so that the sinful body might be destroyed, and we might no longer be enslaved to sin. For he who has died is freed from sin. But if we have died with Christ, we believe that we shall also live with him. For we know that Christ being raised from the dead will never die again; death no longer has dominion over him. The death he died he died to sin, once for all, but the life he lives he lives to God. So you also must consider yourselves dead to sin and alive to God in Christ Jesus.

Let not sin therefore reign in your mortal bodies, to make you obey their passions. Do not yield your members to sin as instruments of wickedness, but yield yourselves to God as men who have been brought from death to life, and your members to God as instruments of righteousness. For sin will have no dominion over you, since you are not under law but under grace.

(Romans 6:3–14)

113

1. Temptation comes at difficult times—but it's what you do with those thoughts that counts. The battle is in the mind.

2. Sow a thought, reap an act. Sow an act, reap a habit. Sow a habit, reap a character. Sow a character, reap a destiny.

3. What the devil wants is to deceive us into believing that the thing we desire is good for us.

4. We are subjected to more temptation than the farmer in the Middle Ages. But God has given us extraordinary grace.

5. What counts is what we do when temptation arises.

6. Most of us would have looked at Bathsheba the way David did. But David allowed the thoughts of temptation to sink in, leading to adultery and murder.

7. David had everything, but all Satan needs is a small opportunity. Once we let temptation in, we're in trouble.

8. We have an affection for sin—we don't want to let go. "Lord, get rid of this … but wait a little while."

9. But don't play with temptation. It's a dangerous dance.

10. Some sins you can wrestle with. But the saints tell us that when it comes to sins of the flesh, it's flight, not fight.

11. If you give in on little things, it starts to build.

12. Sin is being marketed to us very effectively in our culture. It's being painted as virtue. We play this game as a culture and as individuals; we live by the line—or move the line. That's relativism. Sin is sin: call it by its name.

13. Sometimes we fail. We are sinners. The Church isn't scandalized by that. We have the Sacrament of Reconciliation so that we can get right with God.

14. We don't realize how subtle temptation is. Sin is no game! We can't play with temptation and not fall into sin.

15. When we pray "Lead us not into temptation," we're asking for the grace to be alert, to be vigilant, and to resist.

16. We need the strength to overcome temptation. We can't do it by ourselves.

17. The power of prayer, the Eucharist, Confession —these all help us overcome temptation.

18. Guys in small groups working together give each other accountability.

19. Satan has a personalized game plan to trap you. The devil has a different strategy for each of us. It's helpful to sit down with a couple of guys you trust and say, "Here's what happens with me."

20. You get out in the light and stop living in the shadows. That's one way of getting power over those habit patterns of sin.

21. We tell young people: "Look out for near occasions of sin. Once you're in there, you lose control."

22. We know where the temptations are. But we go in anyway. We're addicted: we take big risks for small rewards.

23. The issue is virtue and grace; we have to be able to respond to God's call.

TIME OUT

Warm-up questions

1. What particular point(s) caught your attention the most in this segment?

_____

_____

_____

_____

_____

_____

_____

2. What is something useful that you learned from viewing this segment that you can apply in your own life?

_____

_____

_____

_____

_____

_____

_____

Workout questions

1. When we are tempted, what are some of the ways to help prevent us from falling into sin?

_____

_____

_____

_____

_____

_____

_____

2. What is the biggest temptation that you are currently facing? What steps are you taking to help combat this temptation?

_____

_____

_____

_____

_____

_____

_____

3. The Holy Spirit is our protection against the temptation of the devil. What are some other spiritual resources of the Catholic Church that can be helpful to you in avoiding the near occasion of sin?

_____

_____

_____

_____

_____

_____

_____

4. Why is gathering as a group of Christian men on a weekly basis beneficial in the struggle with temptation?

_____

_____

_____

_____

_____

_____

_____

The Lord will fight with you.

➤ Challenge: If you've never opened up your life to another brother, share the truth about your battle with sin.

➤ Remember that the Lord has enough strength and desires to fight for you.

Read the Gospel of John and Proverbs.

➤ Reading good books is another source of encouragement.

➤ Start with Scripture.

➤ Go on to other good books.

➤ Temptation stops 15 minutes after you're in the grave.

➤ The devil is on us 24/7 like a cheap suit.

➤ Run away from temptation. Run to Jesus.

2 Minute Drill:
Personal Fitness Action Plan

Write out an action plan—I commit to becoming spiritually fit by…

NOTES

Deliver Us from Evil

Brian Patrick

PRE-GAME

I'm not ready to join the fight against evil. I'm not a natural leader. I don't speak well. Who's going to listen to me?

Every one of us feels that way sometimes. Sure, we can see that there's a lot of evil in the world. We can see that somebody needs to stand up to it. But does it have to be *me?* I'm no Moses!

But Moses was no Moses, either. When God told him to take up the fight against evil, what was the first thing he said?

> Then the LORD said, "I have seen the affliction of my people who are in Egypt, and have heard their cry because of their taskmasters; I know their sufferings, and I have come down to deliver them out of the hand of the Egyptians, and to bring them up out of that land to a good and broad land, a land flowing with milk and honey, to the place of the Canaanites, the Hittites, the Amorites, the Perizzites, the Hivites, and the Jebusites. And now, behold, the cry of the sons of Israel has come to me, and I have seen the oppression with which the Egyptians oppress them. Come, I will send you to Pharaoh that you may bring forth my people, the sons of Israel, out of Egypt."
>
> But Moses said to God, "Who am I that I should go to Pharaoh, and bring the sons of Israel out of Egypt?"

> He said, "But I will be with you; and this shall be the sign for you, that I have sent you: when you have brought forth the people out of Egypt, you shall serve God upon this mountain."
>
> (Exodus 3:7–12)

"Who am I to stand up against a king?" Moses asked. And God answered him: "But I will be with you."

Throughout the Bible we see the same pattern. God doesn't necessarily look for His servants among the powerful and universally respected. He looks among the shy and humble. Look at Jeremiah, the great prophet who foretold the conquest of Jerusalem:

> Now the word of the LORD came to me saying,
> "Before I formed you in the womb I knew you,
>   and before you were born I consecrated you;
>   I appointed you a prophet to the nations."
> Then I said, "Ah, Lord GOD! Behold, I do not know how to
>   speak, for I am only a youth."
> But the LORD said to me, "Do not say, 'I am only a youth';
>   for to all to whom I send you you shall go,
>   and whatever I command you you shall speak.
> Be not afraid of them,
>   for I am with you to deliver you, says the LORD."
>
> (Jeremiah 1:4–8)

"No one's going to pay attention to me," Jeremiah says. "Oh, but they will," God tells him, "Not because you're somebody special, and not because you're a great speaker, but because *I am with you.*"

That's what we have to remember. When we step up to confront evil, God is with us. We don't have to be brave or smart or important. We just have to have faith. God will take care of the rest.

KICKOFF

1. The devil is a liar, a cheat, a murderer. He's no good.

2. The devil doesn't run around with a pitchfork and a tail. We need to know that he's cunning, tricky, always conniving.

3. Ephesians 6:12: Our battle is with powers and principalities—the real thing—the devil. The devil is real.

4. When Jesus was baptized in the Jordan, the first thing the Spirit did was lead Him into the desert to make spiritual warfare on the devil. The reason He came was to destroy the works of the devil.

5. The world is at war. Are you sitting on the sidelines? Here's how to know: Do you wake up jittery and flustered, like it's right before the big game?

6. If you're not in the fight, then something's wrong.

7. We're afraid to talk about the devil. The consequence of dealing with the devil is eternal damnation.

8. Don't be stupid thinking the devil's not real. If you're going to be delivered from evil, you have to believe there is evil.

9. We need to believe in the devil—and in Jesus' power to conquer the devil, in our lives and the world.

10. Evil is all around us. Without the devil, how else do you explain the reality of persistent evil?

11. We have to understand it and call it by its right name. Then we have to go to war and allow the power of Christ to overcome it.

12. Paranoia—seeing the devil around every corner—is unbalanced, but so is denying his existence.

GAME PLAN

1. 1 John 3:8: "The reason the Son of God appeared was to destroy the works of the devil."

2. Those closest to Jesus were acutely aware of the reality of the devil and spiritual warfare. They saw Jesus sweat blood. They saw Him do battle.

3. Colossians 1:13: "He has delivered us from the dominion of darkness and transferred us to the kingdom of his beloved Son."

4. Colossians 2: We were dead in our sins, but God made us alive by nailing our sins to the Cross.

5. If the devil had known what the Father had planned, he would never have crucified the Lord of glory. He did the one thing he never should have done.

6. Augustine: The flesh of Christ was like the bait on a hook.

127

7.   The devil had each one of us. We had connived with sin. Saying yes to sin produces death.

8.   Jesus deals with our sin by purifying us first, shedding His blood on the Cross.

9.   The devil thought he was triumphing over the Lord. Nailing Him to the Cross should have been the devil's crowning moment.

10.   But as soon as one drop of that precious blood was shed, our sins were cleansed.

11.   That purification enabled us to receive the Holy Spirit. God, who was remote because of our sin, is now able to come near to us and literally live in us as in a temple, making us a new creation. That's how Jesus destroyed the work of the devil.

12.   Psalm 22: Jesus would have memorized it, and saw His own crucifixion spelled out in detail.

13.   The next Psalm is Psalm 23: "The Lord is my shepherd ... Even though I walk through the valley of the shadow of death, I fear no evil; for you are with me."

14.   Christ *is* the Word of God made flesh.

15.   We let the Word of God radiate in our lives—first through the Scriptures, and second through the sacraments.

16.   The Word of God sheds light in our hearts and enables the Lord to heal us.

17.   We have three enemies: the world, the flesh, and the devil.

18.   "The world" means those powers that have turned their backs on Christ.

19.   Christ gives us the power to overcome these enemies and make them serve Christ.

20.   Christ overcame them all. He gives us the power to have His will and His strength against sin. He delivers us from evil.

GAME PLAN SUMMARY

- Remember: The devil is real, and we're at war.

- Our enemies are the world, the flesh, and the devil.

- But through the Word and the sacraments, we can make them serve Christ.

Jesus nailed our bond to the Cross

And you, who were dead in trespasses and the uncircumcision of your flesh, God made alive together with him, having forgiven us all our trespasses, having canceled the bond which stood against us with its legal demands; this he set aside, nailing it to the cross. He disarmed the principalities and powers and made a public example of them, triumphing over them in him.

(*Colossians* 2:13–15)

TIME OUT

Warm-up questions

1. What particular point(s) caught your attention the most in this segment?

_____

_____

_____

_____

_____

_____

2. What is something useful that you learned from viewing this segment that you can apply in your own life?

_____

_____

_____

_____

_____

_____

_____

Workout questions

1. Ephesians 6:12 tells us our struggle is not with flesh and blood but against evil spirits. Why is it impossible to overcome sin and evil without the help of Jesus?

_____

_____

_____

_____

_____

_____

2. Why would Jesus, who is able to conquer all evil, want us, frail and sinful men, to join Him in this battle?

_____

_____

_____

_____

_____

_____

HALFTIME

Jesus told His disciples what was going to happen. If they had just accepted the clear sense of what He said, they would have known everything: "A little while, and you will not see me, and again a little while, and you will see me." But they thought He was talking in riddles.

So Jesus went deeper, and in the process He told them a lot about suffering. The world is full of evil and suffering, but Jesus has overcome the world. Remember that He said this *before* He was crucified! To everyone else, the Crucifixion must have looked like the world overcoming Jesus. But we know it was exactly the opposite. That's why good Christians can be cheerful, even when they're suffering. We know that the victory is won.

"A little while, and you will see me no more; again a little while, and you will see me."

Some of his disciples said to one another, "What is this that he says to us, 'A little while, and you will not see me, and again a little while, and you will see me'; and, 'because I go to the Father'?" They said, "What does he mean by 'a little while'? We do not know what he means."

Jesus knew that they wanted to ask him; so he said to them, "Is this what you are asking yourselves, what I meant by saying, 'A little while, and you will not see me, and again a little while, and you will see me'? Truly, truly, I say to you, you will weep and lament, but the world will rejoice; you will be sorrowful, but your sorrow will turn into joy. When a woman is in labor she has pain, because her hour has come; but when she is delivered of the child, she no longer remembers the anguish, for joy that a child is born into the world. So you have sorrow now, but I will see you again and your hearts will rejoice, and no one will take your joy from you. In that day you will ask nothing of me. Truly, truly, I say to you, if you ask anything of the Father, he will give it to you in my name. Hitherto you have asked nothing in my name; ask, and you will receive, that your joy may be full.

"I have said this to you in figures; the hour is coming when I shall no longer speak to you in figures but tell you plainly of the Father. In that day you will ask in my name; and I do not say to you that I shall ask the Father for you; for the Father himself loves you, because you have loved me and have believed that I came from the Father. I came from the Father and have come into the world; again, I am leaving the world and going to the Father." His disciples said, "Ah, now you are speaking plainly, not in any figure! Now we know that you know all things, and need none to question you; by this we believe that you came from God."

Jesus answered them, "Do you now believe? The hour is coming, indeed it has come, when you will be scattered, every man to his home, and will leave me alone; yet I am not alone, for the Father is with me. I have said this to you, that in me you may have peace. In the world you have tribulation; but be of good cheer, I have overcome the world."

(John 16:16–33)

1. Everybody's dealing with something.

2. Danny dealt with alcoholism—going down the road to destruction.

3. Now he prays and goes to Mass daily and is involved with men's prayer groups. If he didn't do those things, he might be back where he was before.

4. Don't drift with the culture. Stand up and resist. Then the fruits of the Spirit starts to grow in your life.

5. This is the time to fight. The battle is real.

6. We've been told a half-truth our whole lives: "God loves you no matter what." That's true, but …

7. God loves you too much to leave you the way you are. It really does matter what you do.

8. God made you for a purpose. He has roles and responsibilities for you.

9. The Lord taps on our hearts daily. We don't always pay attention. The door only has a doorknob on the inside.

10. We can't beat Satan one on one. We have to bring the Lord into our lives.

11. We're not alone. We have guardian angels and the Holy Spirit. We should be asking for help. When we don't ask for help, we get in trouble.

12. The devil has no hold on Christ, because Jesus never gave in to the temptation.

13. We give the devil access when we say yes to sin. The devil keeps putting the forbidden fruit in front of your face, because he needs you to exercise your freedom to pursue that desire for sin. Once you say yes, you give him a handle—and then another, and another, and another.

14. He wants to lead you to death, despair, and hell. He hates you and me because we're the image of the living God.

15.   But Jesus kicked his rear end. John 16:33: "I have overcome the world." We won. We should be confident. We're guaranteed victory—but only if we fight.

16.   We have angels who are warriors to fight with us.

17.   We need more laborers in the vineyard. Men need to stand up in the Church.

18.   Peter: Resist the devil—he prowls like a lion seeking someone to devour. If you resist, he will flee.

19.   Passivity is our culture. Killing of children, mass-production of pornography—it's all happened while Christian men have sat by and let it happen.

20.   We need to get on our knees in prayer, then out overturning evil in the culture.

21.   Other guys need to lift up the guys on the front lines in prayer.

22.   If you're not a threat, the devil will leave you alone.

23.   You start to learn when the devil is after you.

RED ZONE // RED ZONE

The devil is on the prowl

Be sober, be watchful. Your adversary the devil prowls around like a roaring lion, seeking some one to devour. Resist him, firm in your faith, knowing that the same experience of suffering is required of your brotherhood throughout the world. And after you have suffered a little while, the God of all grace, who has called you to his eternal glory in Christ, will himself restore, establish, and strengthen you.

(1 Peter 5:8–10)

TIME OUT

Warm-up questions

1. What particular point(s) caught your attention the most in this segment?

_____

_____

_____

_____

_____

_____

_____

2. What is something useful that you learned from viewing this segment that you can apply in your own life?

_____

_____

_____

_____

_____

_____

_____

Workout questions

1. What holds you back in the battle against evil? Is it an obstacle within or something on the outside?

_____

_____

_____

_____

_____

_____

2. What can we do to make ourselves more effective weapons in the Lord's battle against evil?

_____

_____

_____

_____

_____

_____

3. In John 16:33, Jesus tells us to "Take courage, He has overcome the world." If we believe this message, what are the ways we are living it out in our daily lives?

_____

_____

_____

_____

_____

_____

4. How can we build one another up as men that we might become a stronger, more unified army of the Lord?

_____

_____

_____

_____

_____

_____

_____

Challenge: Make a decision to get into the fight.

➤ Resist the devil in all the areas the Lord has given you responsibility for.

➤ No more passivity, no more indifference—you're in the game.

Ask God to give you a personalized mission.

➤ The world is at war.

➤ A corner of the battle has your name on it.

➤ Where is the evil that drives you most crazy? Go to war there.

➤ Go to church and go before the Lord and ask for your marching orders.

➤ We're either in a battle with temptation, or coming out, or about to enter.

➤ But the Lord said, "I have overcome the world."

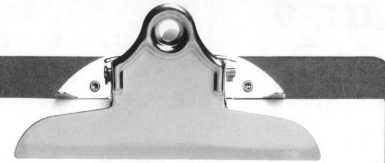

2 Minute Drill:
Personal Fitness Action Plan

Write out an action plan—I commit to becoming spiritually fit by…

NOTES